THE
MEDIEVAL
WORLD

THE

MEDIEVAL WORLD

ANITA BAKER

ANDRE
DEUTSCH

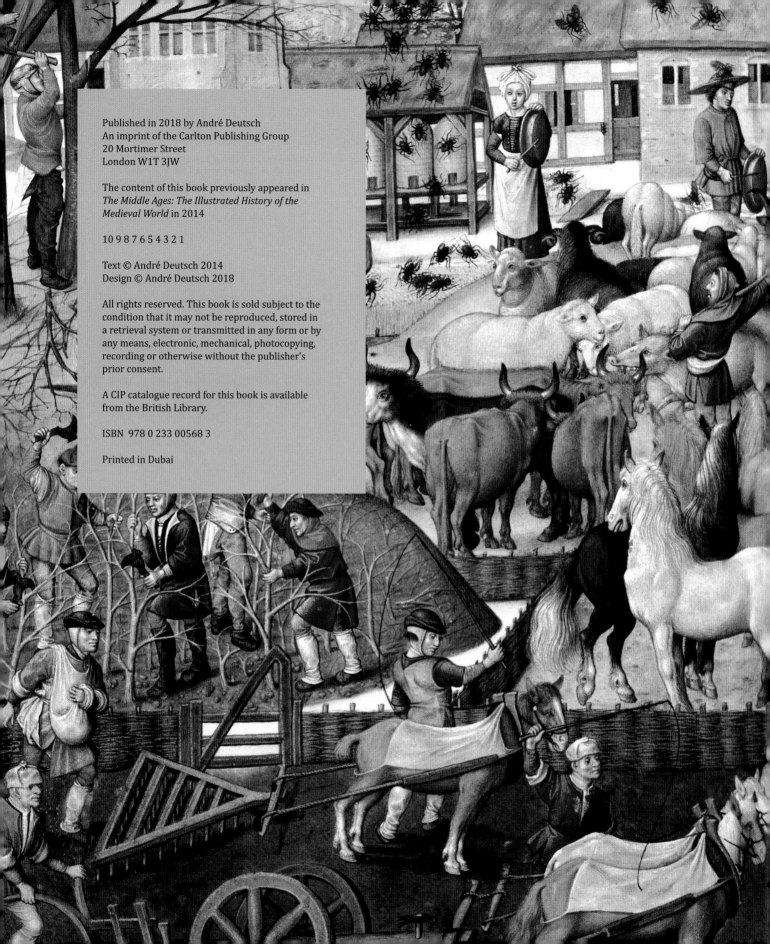

Published in 2018 by André Deutsch
An imprint of the Carlton Publishing Group
20 Mortimer Street
London W1T 3JW

The content of this book previously appeared in
*The Middle Ages: The Illustrated History of the
Medieval World* in 2014

10 9 8 7 6 5 4 3 2 1

Text © André Deutsch 2014
Design © André Deutsch 2018

A CIP catalogue record for this book is available
from the British Library.

ISBN 978 0 233 00568 3

Printed in Dubai

INTRODUCTION

The known world at the start of the Middles Ages consisted of the areas we know of today as Europe, the Middle East and North Africa. Set between the time of the great Roman Empire and the Renaissance of the fifteenth and sixteenth centuries, the Middle Ages is often said to cover the period between the end of the Western Roman Empire in 476 and the capture of Constantinople by the Ottomans in 1453, which signified the fall of the Byzantine Empire.

BELOW The Battle of Montgisard on 25 November 1177 was one of Saladin's most crushing defeats at the hands of the crusader forces. The Knights Templar, fighting alongside Baldwin IV, the leper king, played a significant part in the battle.

OPPOSITE The Battle of Hastings, which took place on the 14 October 1066.

However, in England the end of the Middle Ages is usually defined by the death of Richard III at the Battle of Bosworth and the start of the Tudor dynasty in 1485. This will be the date used in this book to signify the end of the period.

To understand the situation in Europe at the start of the Middle Ages it is necessary to look at what led to the fall of half of the great Roman Empire. In 375, the Roman Empire had been divided into the Eastern and Western Empires. The capital of the Eastern, or Byzantine, Empire was Constantinople, and Ravenna became the administrative capital of the Western Empire in 402 when the imperial court moved there. By the early years of the fifth century, the Western Roman Empire had already begun its decline. It seemed to be under attack from all sides. The Vandals were razing Gaul, making their way down through the Empire to North Africa, and the Visigoths had invaded Italy, sacking Rome in 410.

The Eastern Empire was also not without its own problems. Towards the middle of the century it was at war with the Huns, and although the Hun armies eventually returned to their own territory, they took with them a huge amount of plunder and left behind devastated cities and a defeated Roman Army. The Huns did not leave the Western Empire unscathed either. They invaded Gaul in 451, but were beaten back at the Battle of Châlons. Not deterred, they then invaded Italy over the Alps, destroying city after city in a country already broken by famine. Without the supply chain needed to take Rome, they eventually retreated again, leaving devastation in their wake. Fortunately, before any more planned attacks could take place, in 453 Attila, the great leader of the Huns, died, leaving the empires free from further Hunnic attacks.

However, with the death of Attila, Rome was still not safe. At the time of his death, the Vandals held much of Rome's former territory in North Africa and the Mediterranean and, with it, great wealth. In 455 they sacked Rome under the pretence of rescuing the late Emperor Valentinian III's widow from an unwanted marriage and left with her, her daughters and many riches. Though both Roman empires eventually retaliated with an attempted invasion of the Vandal lands in North Africa, their invading fleets were seized or destroyed. Unable to retake the lands, in 476 Constantinople agreed a peace with the Vandals. That same year, the Western Roman Emperor, Romulus Augustus, was deposed and Italy, the last remaining territory of the once great Western Roman Empire, became a part of the Eastern Roman Empire ruled by Odoacer, the barbarian, for the Eastern Emperor Zeno.

Thus started the Early Middle Ages. The Western Roman Empire was no more and its former territory was mainly ruled over by a number of Germanic peoples. As seen, the Vandals held parts of northern Africa, including the major trading city of Carthage, and Italy was ruled by Odoacer. The Franks controlled parts of northern Gaul, the Netherlands and Belgium; the Angles, Saxons and Britons held sway over modern day England and Wales and in the mainland territories the Ostrogoths, Thuringians and Alamanni were just a few of the many tribes ruling over the lands of the former empire.

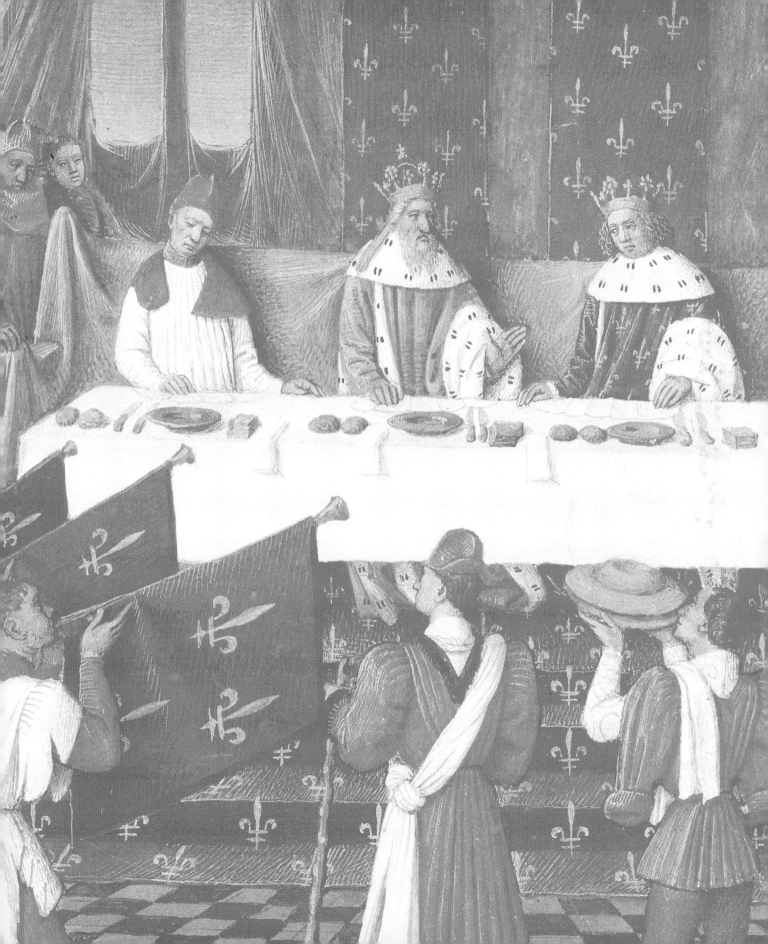

CHAPTER
I

"RIGHT ACTION
IS BETTER THAN
KNOWLEDGE; BUT IN
ORDER TO DO WHAT IS
RIGHT, WE MUST KNOW
WHAT IS RIGHT."

CHARLEMAGNE (c. 742–814)

DYNASTIES
AND EMPIRES

Europe at the start of the Middle Ages

The Salian Franks had lived in the Roman territory known as Toxandria, situated in Holland and Belgium between the River Scheldt and the River Meuse.

They had been allies of the Romans since the middle of the fourth century when they surrendered to the Romans and accepted their terms of settlement. Over the following hundred years, they gradually took more and more land, and by 476 their kingdom covered areas of northern France, the Netherlands and Belgium. A number of other Frankish tribes also controlled various territories around that area.

In 481, upon the death of his father Childeric, Clovis became the king of the Salian Franks and founder of the Merovingian dynasty. He was around 15 years of age. During his reign he brought order and discipline to his army, making them a formidable force. He also succeeded in unifying the Franks under his sole leadership. In 486 he defeated the Roman general Syagrius, who ruled the area around Soissons in northern Gaul. This victory meant that, apart from territory in Italy, the Romans no longer had control over any area of the former Western Empire. Clovis then went on to battle against other Germanic tribes – the Alemanni, the Burgundians and the Visigoths – and successfully expanded his domain to include a large part of Gaul. In 507 his defeat of the Visigoths at the Battle of Vouillé led to the Byzantine Emperor Anastasius giving him authority over Gaul, expanding his territory even further.

One of the most significant events in Clovis' life was his conversion to Catholicism. Unlike the other Germanic kings who mostly converted to Arian Christianity, Clovis converted to Catholicism at around the turn of the century. His conversion was the result of the influence of his wife, Clotilde, a Burgundian princess. His choice of religion meant that the Franks would practise the same religion as the Gallo-Romans living in their kingdom, thus avoiding the religious strife that plagued some of the other Germanic kingdoms. It also meant that Clovis had the support of most of his people, which made his subsequent conquests easier.

On his death in 511, Clovis' kingdom was divided between his four sons and was divided again and again over the years that followed. However, despite this and constant internecine fighting, the Merovingian dynasty continued to rule until 751.

During the first few years of the Middle Ages Odoacer, the king of Italy, expanded his territory by annexing Dalmatia and invading Noricum to the northeast. However, as Odoacer's territory and power grew, Zeno, the Eastern emperor, felt that he had become too much of a threat. Therefore, Zeno promised the kingdom of Italy to the Ostrogoth Theodoric if he could remove Odoacer. After a successful campaign in the north of Italy, Theodoric besieged Ravenna, Odoacer's capital, where he was holding out against the Ostrogoths, for

more than three years. Then in 493 he made peace with Odoacer and they agreed to rule together. It was not to be a long and happy union, though, as two weeks later Theodoric killed Odoacer in his own palace, ironically at a banquet celebrating their union. Theodoric then took control of the kingdom as sole ruler.

As Odoacer had done, Theodoric ruled Italy for the Roman emperor. Most of his rule saw a time of tolerance with Roman living alongside Goth, with each subject to their own laws and customs. Theodoric wanted to re-establish the Western Empire and so he sought alliances through marriage with the western Germanic kingdoms. However, ultimately he was unsuccessful in his aim. His attempt to ally with the western kingdoms brought him the distrust of the Byzantines. This, along with religious differences that had begun to cause conflict among his

subjects, meant that his kingdom was already weakening by the time of his death in 526. After Theodoric's death his young grandson Athalaric became king and the kingdom continued its decline.

In 527, Justinian became Byzantine emperor on the death of his uncle, Justin I. His wife, Theodora, had much influence over him and played an active part in the decisions he made. This is shown by her actions in 532, when the Nika riots broke out in Constantinople, and threatened not only to usurp the government, but also the life of Justinian himself. Justinian was ready to escape with his officials. However, Theodora convinced him to stay and make a stand. On Justinian's command his soldiers quelled the riots, massacring thousands. By using her influence over him Theodora had saved Justinian's reign and she ruled by his side until her death in 548.

Although already at war with Persia when he became emperor, Justinian wanted most to restore the magnificence of the Empire and retake the lands in the west. To this end, he made peace with the Persians in 532 and then turned his attentions westward. First, he attacked the Vandals in North Africa in 533 and reclaimed the land for the Empire.

Next Justinian looked to Italy. Since Theodoric's death, much anti-Byzantine feeling had been shown by a number of the Goths and religious differences were becoming violent between Arian and Catholic. Justinian decided that he needed to exert greater control over the country and to this end he invaded in 536 and by 540 he had established his own government of the country. However, the Ostrogoths were not defeated yet and under the leadership of Totila they went on the offensive in the south of the country. They continued north over the following years until Totila effectively ran the country. However, their success was not to last. In 552 Justinian sent a massive army to retake Italy and the Ostrogoths were defeated at the Battle of Taginae in 552 and the Battle of Monte Lacteria in 553. Although there was resistance for the next decade, by 562 the Byzantines controlled all of Italy. However, despite Justinian's wishes to restore prosperity to Italy and see it thrive once more, Italy had been so devastated by the years of war that it did not prosper and was lost to Lombard invaders in 568, three years after Justinian's death. While Justinian was at war in Italy, hostilities were renewed with the Persians in 540. A truce was eventually agreed in 545 for part of the frontier., but a more permanent truce was not enacted until 562.

The reign of Justinian had brought the Empire to the apex of its power, but it was not without controversy. His insatiable need to regain the lost territories exhausted the wealth of the Empire and he taxed his people heavily to pay for his campaigns, a source of much dissatisfaction. He also left the Empire in a weakened state because, while his attention had been fixed on the west, the borders of the Empire had become an easy target. The Empire was left in no position to fight off an invasion from a new adversary when it came and, thus, the rise of Islam and the Muslim invasions of the following centuries saw the Empire greatly diminished.

Justinian should not be remembered just for his wars, however. He was also a great patron of the arts and built many structures, including churches, fortresses and aqueducts. His most impressive work was without doubt the Hagia Sophia in Constantinople. This domed cathedral was the largest cathedral in the world for almost a millennium and an amazing feat of architecture.

One of Justinian's greatest achievements was the *Corpus Juris Civilis*, sometimes known as the *Codex Justinianus* or the Justinian Code. This work was an amalgamation of centuries of jurisprudence, making one body of civil laws that was the sole source of law for the Empire.

ABOVE Justinian is perhaps best remembered for his *Corpus Juris Civilis*, the contents of which has influenced many of the laws that are still in use in Europe today, a millennium and a half after its creation.

The Code was split into four parts. The first was the *Codex Constitutionum*, which contained all the imperial *constitutions*, or legally binding pronouncements, with any contradictory or outdated material taken out. It took a body of ten men two years to put just the Codex together. A revised edition, which included Justinian's new laws, was issued five years later.

The second part of the Code was the *Digesta*. The jurist Tribonian oversaw 16 lawyers who inspected all the writings of all authorized jurists, many from the second and third centuries. Any writings they thought valuable, even if they were simply opinions about legal points, were included and made law. Anything not included was to be considered unenforceable. The *Digesta* was issued in 533 in 50 volumes.

The *Institutiones* was the third part of the Code and was a textbook for new law students. It too was issued in 533 and its compilation was overseen by Tribonian. The final part of the Code was the *Novellae Constitutiones post Codicem*, which contained new laws issued by Justinian after 534.

The Code is of great significance today because during the later Middle Ages it was revived and most Western civil law is in some part based on this rediscovered Roman law.

The Carolingian Dynasty and Charlemagne

The Frankish king who managed to stem the tide of Islamic expansion in western Europe was Charles Martel ("the Hammer"), who was considered by many to be the saviour of western Europe.

Charles Martel was one of the early Carolingians. Although while he was in power the Mergovians were still on the throne, they were puppet kings with little authority. The real power was held by the mayors of the palace, who were originally heads of the royal household, administrators in charge of overseeing palace affairs. Over time they garnered more and more influence until they were the true wielders of power in the kingdom, advising the kings on an array of matters and eventually controlling the government. In Charles' time there were two mayors, one each for the eastern and western kingdoms. Charles' father, Pépin II, was the mayor of the palace in Austrasia, the eastern

kingdom. After Pépin II's death, Charles took power and defeated the western Franks, becoming the sole mayor and thus ruler of the Franks.

Charles' rule was followed by that of Carloman and Pépin, his sons. When Carloman entered a Roman monastery in 747, Pépin became the sole mayor. Because only the pope could sanction the removal of a family as rulers, Pépin petitioned Pope Zachery for permission to remove the powerless Mergovian king and to assume the throne himself. This permission was given and so Pépin became the first Frankish king of the Carolingian dynasty. In return for the throne, Pépin went to war against the Lombards who had seized Ravenna and were preparing to besiege Rome. He gave the pope the territory taken from the Lombards during the conflict and this territory, which included Ravenna, was to become the start of the Papal States, land over which the pope had sovereignty.

RIGHT In 771 Charlemagne repudiated his Lombard wife. He then went on to invade the Lombard lands of his former father-in-law, King Desidarius. On the defeat of Desidarius in 774, Charlemagne had himself crowned king of the Lombards.

When Pépin died in 768 his kingdom was divided between his two sons, Carloman, and perhaps the most famous Frank of them all, Charlemagne. Carloman died in 771, and even though he had two sons, Charlemagne annexed his territories, becoming the sole ruler of the Franks. Charlemagne was a true warrior king whose rule was dominated by war. In 773 he went to war against the Lombards at the request of Pope Adrian I. When the war ended in 774, Charlemagne was victorious. He annexed northern Italy, making it part of the Frankish Empire and became the new king of the Lombards. In 778 he invaded Spain and attempted to take the city of

Saragossa. This battle is immortalized in the epic French poem, the *Song of Roland*. The poem is different from reality because in it Charlemagne is victorious, whereas he was actually beaten by the Basques and returned to his own kingdom.

In 788 Charlemagne annexed Bavaria and forced the ruler to enter a monastery. In the latter years of his reign he fought the Moors in Spain and the Saracens to the south of Italy, where he took Sardinia, Corsica and the Balearic Islands. To the southeast he fought the Avars, claiming huge amounts of booty for his kingdom, and the Slavs who surrendered and went on to become allies.

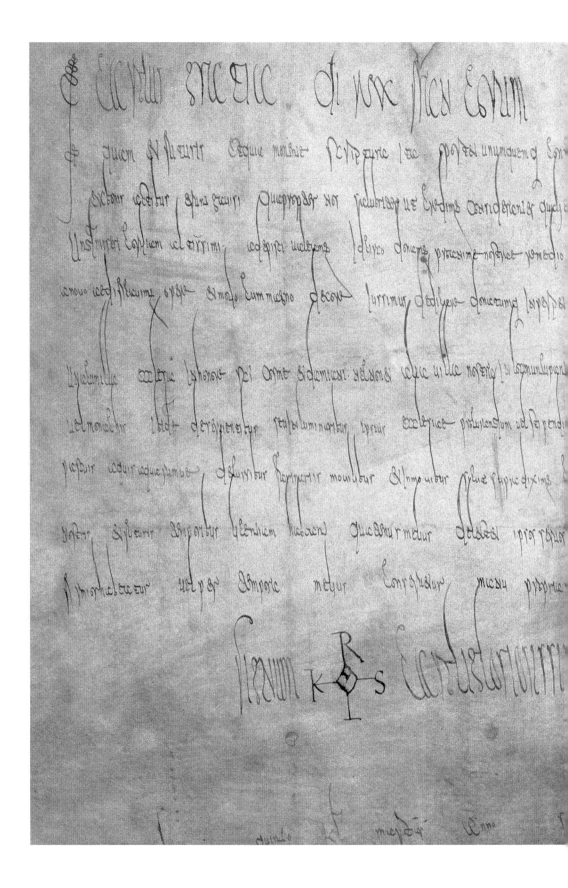

RIGHT A charter issued by Charlemagne, King of the Franks and Emperor of the Romans on 7 January 777 which granted the monastery of Fulda the royal lands of Hammelburg, Eschenbach, Diebach, and Erthat. The monastery had been founded in 744 by Saint Boniface.

While all these other campaigns were taking place, Charlemagne was also fighting an arduous, long-term war with the Saxons. The aim of this war was two-fold. Not only did Charlemagne wish to incorporate the Saxon lands into the kingdom of the Franks, he also wanted to convert the pagan Saxons to Christianity, using force if necessary. The campaign started in 772 and was extremely brutal. Charlemagne instituted laws that made paganism a capital offence, ordering on one occasion the massacre of 4,500 pagans. Although there were periods of peace, the war lasted for 32 years. By its end in 804, the Saxons had renounced their paganism and accepted Christianity and their lands had been incorporated into the kingdom of the Franks.

The war with the Saxons had, to all intents and purposes, been a religious war and, although there was criticism about the way he went about converting the Saxons, the end result met with the approval of the Church. Charlemagne was a deeply religious man and when Pope Leo III was persecuted and deposed by the Romans, it was Charlemagne to whom he went for protection. Once back on the papal throne, Leo crowned Charlemagne as Holy Roman Emperor on Christmas Day in the year 800, thus making him the defender of Rome.

Charlemagne was not just a warrior, he was also a diplomat. As well as using force, he also used diplomacy to maintain his kingdom's status and borders, making allies of a number of his neighbours. He introduced many political reforms and was instrumental in bringing about the Carolingian Renaissance, a cultural revival. He placed great emphasis on education and founded a royal library and palace school and scriptorium at Aachen, his main power base, where a new writing system was developed to make manuscripts easier to read and copy. The palace school was the model for numerous monastic schools across the realm, as Charlemagne had ruled in 789 that all monasteries should have a school in which boys should be educated. Under Charlemagne's rule literature, art and architecture flourished and he was instrumental in incorporating the cultures of other countries into his empire.

A kingdom such as that of Charlemagne needed a strong leader and with Charlemagne's death in 814 that leader was lost. Because of the Frankish tradition of dividing the lands between sons, it did not take long

for the magnificent kingdom of the Franks to fragment and disintegrate and by the late ninth century, the power of the Carolingians was all but gone. However, Charlemagne's legacy, the expansion of Christianity in Europe and the idea of a unified Europe with common religious and political practices, remained.

Europe in the Tenth Century

By the start of the tenth century Europe was at the lowest point of the Middle Ages. The Vikings were raiding and destroying at will (see pages 113–115) and political upheaval and conflict racked the continent. However, the tenth century was to be a century of rebirth when new dynasties were established and power was consolidated.

In the Iberian Peninsula Abd al-Rahman III, the emir of the area, established the Caliphate of Cordoba in 929. Having supressed the Muslim Fatimids in the south and the Christians invading to the north, al-Rahman ruled over a flourishing realm. Throughout the tenth century the Caliphate prospered, with its industry and agriculture regenerated and trade thriving throughout the Mediterranean and beyond. The Great Mosque – which had been originally built in the 780s by Abd Ar-

Rahman, the founder of the Emirate of Cordoba – was enlarged and improved and culture thrived, with a massive library being built in Cordoba. The prosperity of the Caliphate was not to last, however, and the lack of a strong caliph meant that in the early decades of the eleventh century it was immersed in civil unrest and uprising, finally disintegrating in 1031.

The Frankish Kingdom in the tenth century was a weak shadow of its former self. The area now known as Normandy was ceded in 911 to Viking invaders under Rollo, who established the Duchy of Normandy. The eastern Frankish lands were ruled over by the German Ottonian dynasty, the Duchy of Burgundy, was almost completely autonomous and Brittany was totally independent. The Carolingians were still on the throne, but they were weak figureheads. It was not until 987, with the election of Hugh Capet as King of the Franks, that a strong leader sat on the throne and the Carolingians were removed from power permanently. Hugh Capet was the founder of the Capetian dynasty, which would rule for more than 300 years. His descendants gradually increased the size and power of France over the coming centuries.

Tenth-century Germany was stronger than its Frankish neighbour. The Germanic tribes of the eastern Frankish Empire had elected Henry I, Duke of Saxony, as king in 918. He was a strong leader whose successes included negotiating a truce with the Hungarian Magyars, who had invaded in 921. When the truce broke down, Henry defeated the Magyars at the battle of Riade in 933. He also quelled the Slavs to the east. On his death in 936, Henry was succeeded by his son Otto I who, at the start of his reign, put down a number of revolts led by the dukes who ruled over the various German tribes and territories. Once victorious, Otto bestowed all the major German duchies on close relatives so that they could be better controlled. Otto also strengthened and enlarged his kingdom by making gains against the Slavs, subjugating Bohemia, defeating the Magyars and invading Italy, making it a vassal kingdom. In 962 he was made Holy Roman Emperor by Pope John XII, who also made him protector of the Papal States, which had been invaded by Berengar of Ivrea, an Italian noble. Otto went on to retake the Papal

States and, when Pope John XII turned against him, Otto deposed first him and then his successor, Pope Benedict V. The people of Rome were forced to promise not to vote in another pope without the emperor's approval, giving him even more power. Otto died in 973 and was succeeded by his son, Otto II, who carried on his father's work of strengthening the empire, making it a stable power in an unstable world.

Power was shifting in the east as well. At the end of the ninth century Simeon I, leader of the Bulgars, reigned over an expanding Bulgarian Empire which was flourishing not just territorially, but culturally as well. Although peace had prevailed between the Bulgarian and Byzantine Empires during the reign of Simeon's father, problems with trade in Byzantium led Simeon to invade. The Byzantines foiled his invasion by making a pact with the Magyars to the north of Bulgaria who invaded, thus diverting Simeon's attention away from Byzantium. However, the Magyars were eventually defeated and Simeon once again marched south. Throughout the early years of the tenth century, until Simeon's death in 927, Bulgaria and Byzantium clashed on and off, with Byzantium ceding much territory to the Bulgars. However, on Simeon's death, a peace was wrought between the two parties with Peter I, the new leader of the Bulgars, marrying the Byzantine emperor's daughter. This peace was to last almost 40 years until the two empires again went to war. Eventually, in 1014, the Byzantines were victorious and the Bulgar lands became part of the Byzantine Empire.

For the first time England, bar a few areas that were still under Viking control, was united under one Anglo-Saxon king. However, towards the end of the century this unity was threatened when the throne was taken by Aethelred II, more popularly known as Aethelred the Unready. Under his long, 38-year rule, the Vikings took more and more territory and England once more became a bloody battlefield (see pages 113–115).

Going into the new millennium new kingdoms had been formed and old ones were weakening or had disappeared. With the Christianization of much of Europe, the papacy was garnering more power and feudalism was prominent across the continent. Thus began the High Middle Ages.

The Angevin kings of England

When Henry II succeeded King Stephen of England in 1154 he was already Duke of Normandy, Duke of Aquitaine – because of his marriage to Eleanor of Aquitaine, who had brought to the marriage her vast, rich lands in southwest France – and Count of Anjou, Maine and Touraine.

One of his first achievements was the restoration of the lands in the north of England lost by Stephen to the Scottish. Then in 1166 he conquered Brittany, making him the ruler of a domain that reached from the northern borders of Normandy to the Pyrenees and to the Scottish border. This huge expanse of territory brought with it many riches and made Henry one of the wealthiest men in Europe.

Henry not only expanded his territory during his reign, but he proved himself an able, if unpopular, ruler and politician. He restored order to an England that had become increasingly lawless during Stephen's reign and reformed the judicial system. However, despite his successes, his rule will always be remembered for one thing above all else – the murder of Thomas Becket. Becket was the Archbishop of Canterbury and he seemed to oppose Henry at every turn. Things came to a head when, after returning to England from exile on the continent, Becket started to cause trouble again. On hearing of this, Henry said the immortal words "Will no one rid me of this turbulent priest?" Four of his loyal knights took his words to heart and sped off to Canterbury where, on 29 December 1170, they slaughtered Becket in the cathedral. However, the murder of Becket did little to truly damage Henry's rule.

ABOVE Henry I defeated the Magyars at the battle of Riade in 933, ending their devastating raids on the German countryside.

RIGHT Aethelred II, commonly known as Aethelred the Unready.

BELOW Otto I was crowned Holy Roman Emperor in 962. This crown made for his coronation was encrusted with precious stones and pearls and was the imperial crown until the end of the Holy Roman Empire in 1806.

The real damage done during his reign was caused by his sons. Their rebellions marred the final years of his regime and he died an almost broken man in 1189.

Henry was succeeded by his eldest living son, Richard the Lionheart, who became Richard I of England. Richard inherited all of Henry's lands bar Brittany, which went to his brother Geoffrey's son Arthur, and Ireland which, along with various minor holdings, went to his brother John. However, Richard did not stay long to oversee his new lands. In July 1190 he set out on crusade and did not again see England until 1194. He should have been home a year earlier but was taken prisoner on the return journey and held by Henry VI, Holy Roman Emperor. He was released only upon payment of, quite literally, a king's ransom – the huge

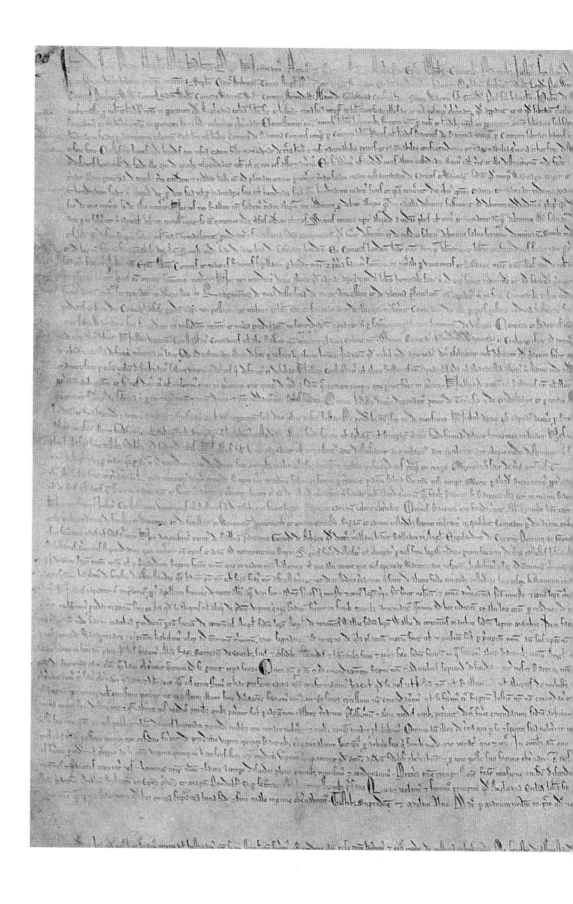

OPPOSITE King
John signs the
Magna Carta,
15 June 1215.

RIGHT Although
Otto I was crowned
Holy Roman
Emperor by Pope
John XII, he later
deposed both him
and his successor
Pope Benedict V.

FAR RIGHT Hugh
Capet was crowned
in 987 at Noyon in
northern France.
His Capetian
dynasty ruled
France for more
than 300 years and
his descendants
sat on the throne
for more than 800
years, albeit with a
few interruptions.

sum of 100,000 marks, which was two-thirds of the ransom demanded by Henry.

While Richard was in prison, Philip II of France had taken advantage of his absence to occupy many of Richard's holdings in France. Richard, therefore, spent the final five years of his reign fighting to take back his lands from Philip. He was successful in this endeavour and managed to regain almost all lost territory. Richard was wounded in March 1199 during the siege of Chalus-Chabrol, where he was fighting a rebellion. He died a couple of weeks later from his wound. The great warrior who had survived the horrors of the Holy Land and imprisonment in Germany was finally felled by a single crossbow bolt in his own land.

Upon his death Richard's lands were split between his brother John, who inherited England and Normandy, and his nephew Arthur, who inherited Brittany, Anjou, Maine and Touraine. John's mother, Eleanor, ruled Aquitaine on his behalf. By 1200 John had taken possession of all of Arthur's territories,

though he had to cede land to Philip II in return for recognition of John's possession of the land. However, John was not to enjoy possession of his lands for long. His marriage to Isabella of Angoulême led to her jilted betrothed appealing to Philip of France. Philip's response was to confiscate all of John's holdings in France, which were technically held as fiefs under the French crown. The ensuing war saw John lose his continental territories and retreat over the Channel to England.

John was determined to regain his lost land. To this end he instigated crippling taxes to fund the war. Added to that, John also argued with the Church to such an extent that in 1209 he was excommunicated. From 1208 all church services in England were stopped on the orders of the pope. John's reaction to this was to seize Church lands and their revenues for himself. The state of affairs lasted until 1213, when John agreed to become a papal vassal and pay tribute. John's actions made him a very unpopular ruler. His further attempts to reclaim

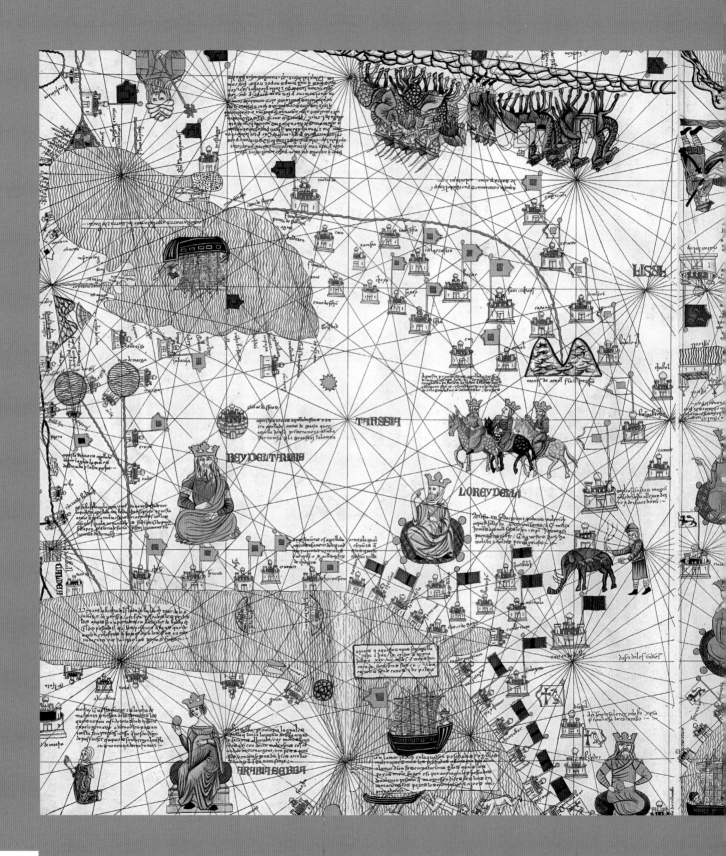

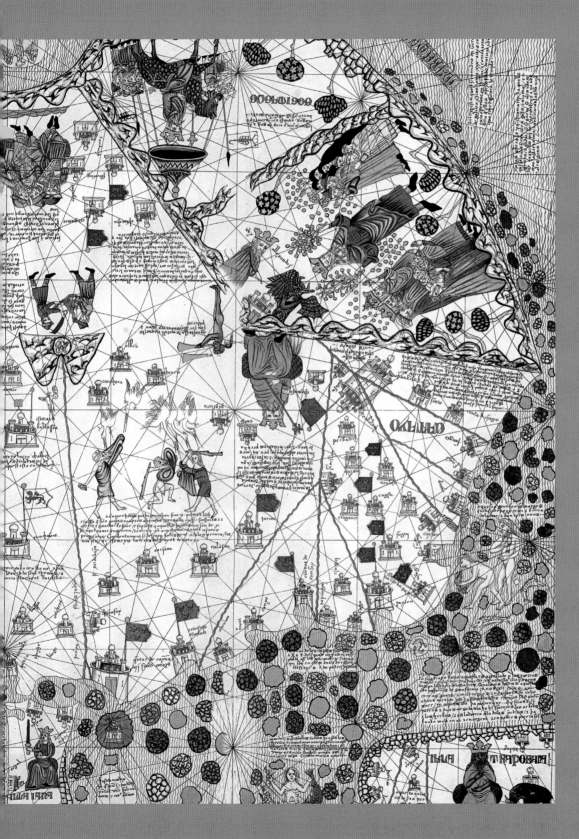

FAR LEFT The murder of St Thomas à Becket as it appears in the *St Alban's Chronicle*. Although the murder was the tragic result of a misunderstanding, it cannot be denied that it left Henry free from the "turbulent priest".

LEFT Frederick I Barbarossa, Holy Roman Emperor, depicted in a 13th-century chronicle.

his continental possessions in 1214 ended in failure and were the final straw for his discontent subjects. His barons rebelled and, in June 1215, John was forced to accept their terms, granting them certain liberties and legal rights. He signed a document, known as the *Articles of the Barons*, laying out these terms on the island of Runnymede in the Thames. The document went through a number of revisions and, in July, the formal document was produced and copies were distributed throughout England. It is this document that would later become known as the Magna Carta.

John, however, had no intention of honouring the terms of the charter. This led to his rebellious barons allying with Louis, the son of Philip of France. Louis invaded England in 1216, and a civil war followed, one that was to continue after John's death in October 1216. It finally ended in September 1217, when the Treaty of Lambeth was signed, ushering in a more peaceful time for England.

The Italian City States

In the tenth century the kingdom of Italy (what is today northern Italy) had become a vassal state of the Holy Roman Empire. The cities in the north of Italy operated in a different way from those in the rest of Europe. Although they were part of the Holy Roman Empire, they ran themselves mostly autonomously. These city states were powerful players on the international stage, in no small part owing to their commercial enterprises.

However, Holy Roman Emperor Frederick I tried to impose his authority over the city states and implement a tax on Italian citizens. The cities responded by forming the Lombard League in 1167. This coalition, which included Venice, Padua and Milan, would eventually number 20 cities. The League was victorious against the emperor in the Battle of Legnano in 1176, forcing him to eventually agree to the Peace of Constance which, while

London : Wm Heinemann.　　　　Printed by the Bibliographisches Institut Leipzig　　　　New York : Dodd, Mead & Co

retaining the fealty of the cities, made Frederick give the cities political and financial freedom.

By the time of the Lombard League a number of the Italian cities, such as Venice, Pisa and Genoa, were already thriving maritime republics. These republics built up fleets of ships which were used for transport and war. The crusades brought them the opportunity to sell provisions and sea transport to the crusaders and, more importantly, they opened up new trade routes and expanded existing ones. The republics established trading communes in the Holy Land, further enhancing trade opportunities. By the end of the thirteenth century the Italian city states had established trading monopolies, especially to the east. Their trading routes took them throughout the Mediterranean and into the Islamic world and even as far as the Mongol Empire. With most merchandise to and from the east going through Italy, it had become the centre of

international trade and some of the city states, such as Venice, were among the wealthiest in Europe.

By the middle of the thirteenth century the Lombard League had split up. In 1250 their last adversary, Holy Roman Emperor Frederick II, who, like his grandfather Frederick I, had tried to impose imperial authority on northern Italy, died. With his death the necessity for the League vanished. The Italian city states, instead of being joined against a common enemy, were now more often in competition with each other. This led to ever shifting cooperation and conflict between the various states; almost as soon as the Lombard League disbanded, Venice and Genoa were at war with each other.

The city states were not only at war with each other, they were also often riven with internal conflict. Different factions within the states, often based on family ties, were frequently involved in power struggles and vendettas that undermined the strength of the city

ABOVE A map showing the extent of the Hanseatic League in about 1400.

state as a whole. These internal power struggles led to most of the states becoming governed by signori during the fourteenth century. Rather than being a republic, the state would be run by a government ruled over by one lord, the signore, who was often chosen for the task because of his strength of character and his ability to maintain law and order. Over time the signori of various states extended their power and made their role hereditary, sometimes even buying an hereditary title, such as a dukedom, to further consolidate their power. During the first half of the fifteenth century Italy was almost continually involved in conflict. The signori of the stronger city states, such as Milan and Florence, expanded their domains by taking over the smaller, weaker city states. To this end they often employed mercenaries, known as *condotierri*, and their armies to fight their innumerable wars for them.

Milan was a major protagonist during that time. In the late fourteenth century the first of a number of wars between Florence and Milan broke out. Florence felt threatened by Milan's territorial conquests, with good reason, as by 1402 the territories held by Milan completely surrounded Florence. Whether Milan would have gone on to take Florence next is unknown because Gian Galeazzo Visconti, the charismatic and ruthless signore of Milan, died in 1402 and his weak son was not able to hold on to the conquests. However, in 1412, another of Gian's sons became signore and restored much of the territory lost under his brother, causing renewed conflict with Florence, now allied with Venice.

Venice also decided to expand on the mainland during the fifteenth century. The alliance with Florence helped with Venice's expansion and it came to rule a large stretch of profitable, fertile land called the Veneto. However, the alliance was not to last and in the middle of the century Florence switched its allegiance to Milan. This change in ally was typical of the city states, which were preoccupied, above all things, with self-interest.

In 1454 Milan, Florence, Naples, the Papal States and Venice allied with each other in a treaty known as the Peace of Lodi. The aim was to maintain the balance of power and to provide defence for all parties. This ushered in a more peaceful time, although there were still conflicts between various states.

The Italian city states were not the only powerful commercial bodies of the Middle Ages. In northern Germany another powerful coalition of traders was formed that would influence trade in northern Europe for centuries. In the early thirteenth century north German traders were already in the habit of joining together to combat pirates and bandits and in the mid-thirteenth century these informal associations started to become official. By the late thirteenth century cities and towns in the north of Germany had formed the Hanseatic League. The League not only set out to protect its merchants, but also to control trade in the north of Europe. To this end it founded permanent trading centres in cities across northern Europe, such as Bruges and London, and set out to gain trade monopolies. Throughout the next century the League went from strength to strength. It protected its commercial interests by bribing foreign leaders with gifts. If that didn't work, the League was not above putting embargoes in place or even going to war to

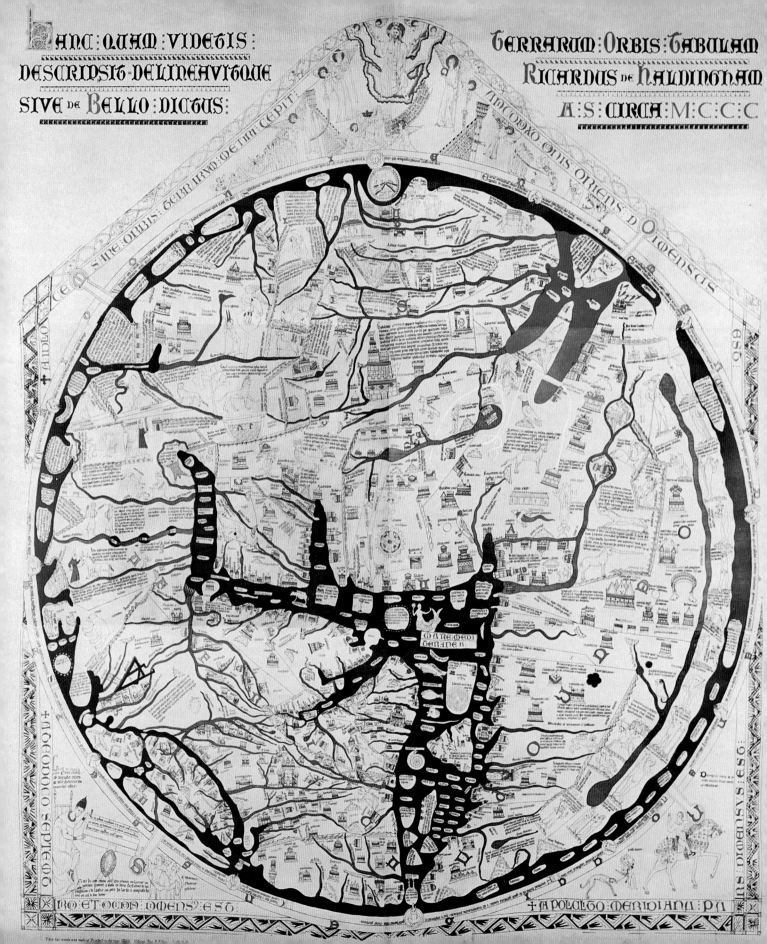

OPPOSITE This is the largest surviving map dating from the Medieval period. It dates from approximately 1285 and appears to be signed by Richard of Haldingham and Lafford. In it can be seen 420 towns, 15 events from the Bible, 33 animals, 32 people and five depictions of classical mythology. At the centre of the map is Jerusalem, east is at the top, Europe in the bottom left and Africa appears on the right. In a circle on the edges of the world is the garden of Eden.

RIGHT The Battle of Legnano, fought on 29 May 1176 was a decisive victory for the Lombard League, destroying Frederick's rule over Lombardy. The Battle of Legnano resulted in the defeat of Emperor Frederick Barbarossa. The success of the League can be put down to a combination of their larger army and the use of well-coordinated infantry and cavalry tactics.

safeguard its interests. Despite its strength, towards the end of the Middle Ages the League began to decline, mainly because of increased competition from other countries. The last official meeting of the League was held in 1669.

The Medici family were the rulers of Florence for almost 300 years. Although originally from peasant stock, they had become members of Florence's elite by the fourteenth century. Giovanni di Bicci de' Medici is considered the first eminent Medici. He founded the Medici bank, which brought him great wealth that he passed on to his children. His son, Cosimo, became the ruler of Florence in 1434. From that time the Medici would be the hereditary heads of the state. As the most powerful family in Florence the Medici gained great wealth and status. Members of the family went on to be popes, royalty and great statesmen. Some family members, such as Lorenzo de' Medici, were great patrons of the arts and supported artists such as da Vinci and Botticelli. There was another side to their privileged lives, though. The Medici lived in a time of corruption, political machination and danger. Rival factions sought to diminish their power and many plotted against them. There were a number of assassination attempts, some successful, over the years and two periods of exile. However, despite all the efforts of their enemies, the Medici dynasty did not collapse until the eighteenth century.

The Rise of the Ottoman Empire

One of the most powerful empires in the world was the Ottoman Empire, which originated in Anatolia. Turkish tribes had taken eastern and central Anatolia from the Byzantine Empire in the twelfth century. They were, themselves, invaded by the Mongols in the thirteenth century and lost their hold on much of eastern Anatolia. By the end of that century, the remaining Turkish-held Anatolia had developed into a number of autonomous principalities. One of these, on the Byzantine border, was ruled by Osman I (from which the name Ottoman derives).

During the fourteenth century Osman wished to expand his Islamic territory, with his natural target being

Christian Byzantium. Osman and his successors, Orhan and Murad I, conquered not only western Anatolia, but also Byzantine lands in southeast Europe. Gallipoli in the Crimea, from where incursions into Europe could be launched, was taken in 1354. The Byzantine city of Adrianople was then conquered in 1361 and turned into the new Ottoman capital. It was renamed Edirne and, because of its position, this strategic city was perfectly placed to aid invasions to the north.

Orhan's son, Murad I, was responsible for Balkan invasions, conquering Bulgaria and most of Serbia in the 1380s. After Murad's death at the Battle of Kosovo in 1389 his successor, his son Bayezid I, was forced to leave Europe and return to Anatolia to deal with threats there. Having put down a revolt in Anatolia, he was faced with another in the Balkans. Once that too had been dealt with successfully, his next challenge was to overcome a crusade against him that had been organized by Hungary. His decisive victory over the crusaders at the Battle of Nicopolis secured his position in Europe. It seemed the Ottomans were unstoppable. However, Europe was to receive temporary relief from the encroaching Ottoman Empire. In 1402 Tamerlane, the great Turkic conqueror, who subjugated most of central Asia and founded the Timurid Dynasty, invaded Anatolia, defeated Bayezid's army and took him prisoner. Bayezid died in captivity.

Tamerlane did not keep Anatolia, but divided it among the Turks who had helped him against the Ottomans. From 1402 until 1413 Bayezid's four sons vied to rule the remaining Ottoman Empire, with Mehmed I being finally victorious. Both he and his son, Murad II, carried on the expansion of Ottoman territory. Between them they reclaimed most of the land lost with Bayezid's defeat and added to it. In 1423 Murad went to war with Venice, which wished to protect their trade routes from Ottoman expansion. In 1432 the Venetians were forced to make peace with the Ottomans and it was agreed that they would stop resistance to the empire and would be given commercial powers in exchange.

Another crusade was launched against the Ottomans in 1444. However, it also failed and the crusaders were crushed at Varna in November of that year. Murad's son, Mehmed II, became sultan in 1451. Like the sultans before him, he was keen to expand the empire. His first objective was the great walled city of Constantinople, the seat of Byzantine power. In May 1453, after a siege that lasted almost two months, Constantinople was finally his. The Byzantine Empire was no more. Mehmed renamed the captured city Istanbul and established a new Ottoman capital there. He turned many of the city's churches, including the magnificent Hagia Sophia, into mosques and built a new palace for the Ottoman sultans.

At the height of its power, in the fifteenth and sixteenth centuries, the Ottoman Empire was incredibly powerful. It included vast areas of southeast Europe, the Middle East and North Africa. Although diminished over the centuries, the Ottoman Empire would exist for more than 600 years until its ultimate demise in 1922.

One of the things that contributed to the success of the Ottoman Empire was its system of Devşirme. Under this system a selection of non-Muslim youths, between the ages of about eight and 20, from conquered territories – mainly the Balkans – would be taken away from their families and placed in the service of the sultan. The "collection" of the boys happened about once every five years or so. There were exemptions, including only children, those from large cities and Jews. Even though a child would possibly never see his family again, it was not unusual for parents to request that their children be taken, as a whole world of opportunity would be open up to them. The boys would convert to Islam and be educated and trained. Depending on their strengths, they would go into administrative, religious or military roles. The brightest would end up in the sultan's palace, where they could be destined for greatness, as the astute could rise up through the ranks of government. Those who joined the infantry were known as Janissaries. The early Janissaries were slaves captured during war. However, by the fifteenth century, they were recruited using the Devşirme system. They were trained to be elite troops who were disciplined and loyal to the sultan. Under Murad II and Mehmed II the Devşirme men gained ever-increasing power. They were rewarded for service with conquered lands and so encouraged further conquest. Eventually, they became some of the most powerful figures in the empire, pushing out the Turkish elite. Although the Devşirme system began to decline during the sixteenth century, it was not until the seventeenth century that it was finally officially ended.

RIGHT In 1453, Sultan Mehmed II besieged Constantinople. The defenders bravely held out against his vastly superior force for almost two months. However, constant hammering by the Ottoman siege engines had seriously weakened the city walls and, eventually, the defenders were no longer able to defend the breaches and the city fell, signalling the end of the once great Byzantine Empire.

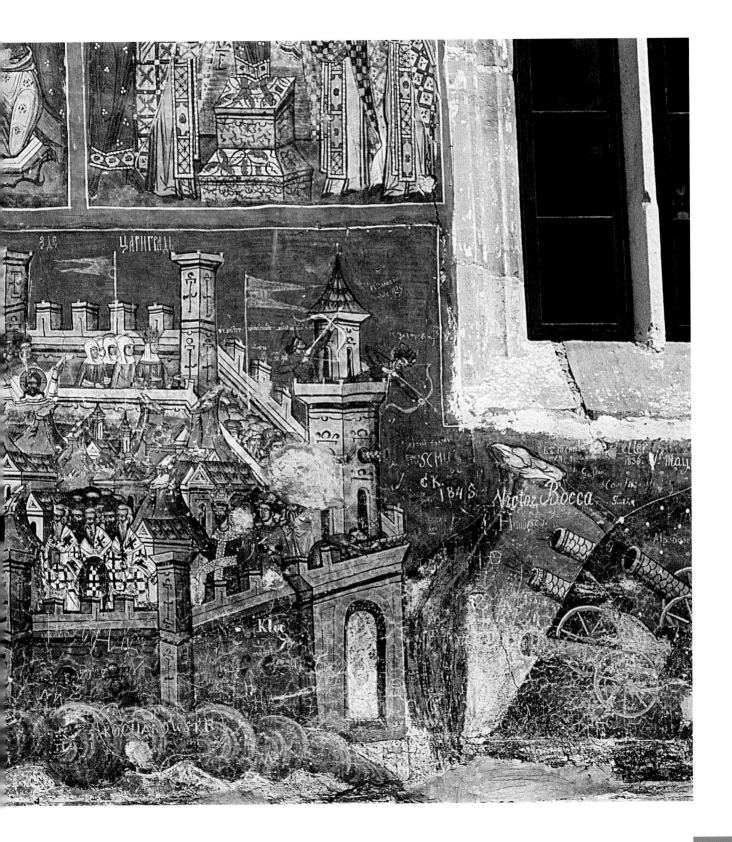

CHAPTER

2

"THE NOURISHMENT OF
BODY IS FOOD, WHILE
THE NOURISHMENT OF
THE SOUL IS FEEDING
OTHERS."

**HAZRAT ALI IBN ABI TALIB
(601–661)**

DAILY LIFE

Feudalism

Feudalism was a form of society that was prevalent in the High Middle Ages. It had been in use in a basic form in some areas of continental Europe as far back as the time of Charles Martel (see pages 14–15), who was instrumental in developing the system.

William the Conqueror was responsible for bringing feudalism to England (see pages 115–119), as the system was an ideal way to rule a conquered land; it would also have been the method of organization that he was used to as the Normans lived in a feudal society.

The feudal system worked on a very simple premise – the granting of land for services. The ruler of the territory, such as a king or a lord, would own all the land. He would keep a proportion of the land for himself and would grant parcels of land to vassals. In return, the vassal would perform services, often of a military nature, for the ruler. To become a vassal, the recipient of the land would have to swear a sacred oath of fealty and pay homage to the ruler granting the land. Should the oath of fealty ever be broken, it was considered a terrible crime.

Vassals were sometimes granted huge amounts of land, as in England under William I, and in return they would be responsible for a large military obligation. To fulfil this obligation they would split the land up into "knight's fees", or fiefs, and grant them to lower vassals, again in return for military service. This pyramid system meant that the king would have a large body of men obliged to fight for him when the need arose. From the twelfth century the holders of fiefs could pay scutage, a monetary sum, instead of having to render the military service owed.

Under the feudal system, as well as providing a stipulated number of men to fight for him, vassals would have other obligations to their lord or king. They would have to swear loyalty to him and provide him with a place to stay and provisions should he visit. Often there were other obligations as well, such as attendance at the lord's court or the obligation to pay ransom should the lord be taken prisoner. Vassals could even have to contribute to the cost of the wedding of their lord's daughter or to the cost of other important events.

In a feudal society the system of reciprocal grants and obligations went lower than the ruling classes and affected the peasants as well. Fiefs were frequently called manors and would often consist of a manor house or castle, fields, pastures, woods and at least one village, which might contain a church. These manors were organized using a system that has come to be called manorialism, which was very similar in structure to the feudal system. Some of the land would be granted out to freemen in return for rent or service. The rest of the land would be held by the lord. Most manors would have had peasants tied to them under the condition called serfdom. In return for protection and land that

BELOW The life of the peasant was hard. However, there was some respite in the form of holy days (holidays) when there would be entertainment and dancing and rest.

they could use for their own subsistence, the serfs were obliged to work for the lord, often on his land, for a certain number of days of each year. They were also obliged to pay certain dues, which would often be paid in produce rather than money.

Although there would be some free peasants working for the lord, the majority would be bonded to the land and every aspect of their lives would be ruled by the lord. They were considered unfree and were not allowed to leave the land without permission. They also needed the lord's permission to marry and had to make payment to the lord upon their marriage. Should ownership of the manor change, the peasant were still not allowed to leave the manor, but simply worked for the new lord.

During the Late Middle Ages feudalism began to decline. There are many reasons for this decline,

including the fact that economies were becoming more money- than land-based. Also, the Black Death massively reduced the population of Europe, leaving fewer peasants to labour on the land, making them more valuable. Other factors were the increase in travel and trade and centralized governments. However, the one reason that stands out is the rise of the standing army. During the later Middle Ages there was an increase in the number of mercenaries available for hire and many kings chose these professional soldiers instead of relying on their vassals. Eventually, it became necessary for kings to employ professional, trained soldiers to combat the threat of mercenaries hired by their enemies, thus negating the need for the military service rendered under the feudal system.

Women in the Middle Ages

Though women did not partake in military service the life of a woman in the middle ages was not an easy one. Although the quality of life for the Middle Ages woman could differ dramatically depending on her situation and class, all women were generally seen as inferior to men and many restrictions were placed upon them. Should a girl survive her birth and infancy, no mean feat in the Middle Ages, then she was destined for an adult life befitting her class. A young noblewoman's lot was often that of a pawn, used by the men in her life to either secure wealth or political position.

Women could be betrothed at a very young age, sometimes even at birth. Adulthood started early; girls were considered of marriageable age at 12 and many noblewomen were married by 14, though the marriage would not be regarded as legal until consummated and it could be annulled before then if necessary. Women would have very little say in the choice of their husband and most marriages were motivated by greed, politics or status. Although women could legally inherit property and wealth, this was usually controlled by the men in their life – either their father or, if he were dead, a guardian. Being the guardian of a wealthy woman was a much sought-after position because the guardian had control over the woman's fortune until she married and he was therefore in a position to choose her husband. Although some noblewomen, such as Eleanor of Aquitaine and the Empress Matilda, came to have great power in their own right, this was a rare occurrence.

Once married, the wife of a lord would settle into a life ruled by him. Everything she had was his and she could do little without his consent. Should he die, she was entitled to her dower, or share of his estate. However, she would become a ward of court and usually be married again, securing her wealth for another man.

The noblewoman did however play a significant role in the running of her home. While the lord was away, she would run the castle or manor and estate, making the necessary legal and financial decisions. She was also responsible for looking after the comfort and entertainment of guests and overseeing the household servants and provisions. She had many responsibilities and was also expected to look fine, with her appearance matching her status.

Should a woman of the upper classes not marry, then the only other acceptable option open to her was to enter a convent. Life as a nun in the convent would be one of work, prayer and study. However, not all who entered the convent became nuns. There are many instances of convents being used as medieval boarding houses for widows and others.

The lot of the peasant woman was vastly different from that of the noblewoman. A peasant girl would marry later in life, usually in her late teens or early twenties, and often had a say in her choice of husband. She married later because she would often work until marriage and marriage would leave her family without a worker. Once married, the peasant woman would do chores with her husband – for example, tilling the fields, planting or harvesting. She could also do paid work, such as labouring or washing, for others. Although often doing the same work as a man, a woman would be paid significantly less.

She would also be responsible for the care of the children, upkeep of the house and all that entailed, making and mending clothes, tending the vegetable patch and cooking the food over an open fire. Life was hard and life expectancy was short.

Between the noblewomen and the peasants there were the middle-class women – the burghers' wives and daughters. These free townswomen would run their household and, along with their servants, would be responsible for all household chores, which would include obtaining provisions, cooking, cleaning and tending the garden. They would also often work alongside their husband or father in their trade. If they were widowed, then the women could run a business left to them by their husbands as long as the relevant guild allowed it.

No matter of what their station in life, most women in the Middle Ages had one thing in common – childbirth. One of the main reasons for marriage was to produce children and women were expected to have numerous children because infant mortality was high. As was usually the case in the Middle Ages, a wealthy woman had more chance of survival than a poor woman, thanks to better cleanliness in the lying-in room where the birth took place, better diet and better care and equipment. There was no effective pain relief that could be used during childbirth and the risk of complications was great, childbirth being the most common cause of death for young women. Most births would be overseen by a midwife, no matter what the rank of the mother. Apart from a male physician in wealthier households, men were banned from the lying-in room. It would be a hot place with a roaring fire to heat water and sometimes many women, including the mother's friends and relatives, would be present. Should the birth go well, the

midwife would cut the umbilical cord, wash and swaddle the baby. Should the birth not go well, the child would be baptized immediately, sometimes by the midwife who was given special dispensation to perform this rite. If the mother died during childbirth, then the midwife would often perform a caesarean section and take the baby out so that it could be baptized. Should both the child and mother survive, then childbirth was a time of great joy and celebration.

The Church in Daily Life

Being baptized introduced the child to another important aspect of life in the Middle Ages – the Church. In the Middle Ages the Church and religion played a huge role in almost every aspect of life in Christian Europe. A terror of going to hell was instilled into people at a young age and they would be encouraged to obey the teachings of the Church to secure their place in heaven.

Most peasants would belong to a parish, which could include just their village or a number of villages. Every year, they would pay the parish a tax called a tithe, which amounted to ten per cent of their income. The tithe would often be paid at the parish's tithe barn and many would only be able to pay it in kind by supplying grain or animals in place of coin. For the poor peasants, this was a substantial burden to bear, but most paid the tithe even if it would lead to great hardship.

A parish would be presided over by a parish priest and all tithes would go to him, usually to be split between his own pocket and the church. In the early years, the priest was generally appointed by the Lord of the manor and housed by the Lord. However, in the later Middle Ages the lord would grant the priest the parish as a "living". Some priests would have more than one living and would pay another to take over the duties in the parish in which they did not reside. The revenues from the parish would still go to the original holder of the living. The man actually fulfilling the role of parish priest would often be of a lower rank, whereas the priest who had the living was often the younger son of a nobleman.

Priests would not earn money just from the tithe, but from other sources as well. The living would come with land called a "glebe", which the priest could work himself or rent out to gain revenue. He was also paid for his services since donations were made for such things as baptisms and weddings. There were also other minor

Many castles and manor houses had their own private chapels and a chaplain would be employed to serve the lord and his family. The chaplain would say mass for the household and perform weddings, christenings and funerals for the family. He would also travel with them, if required, seeing to their religious needs while away from home. Again, especially in the Early Middle Ages, the chaplain would often be the only literate member of the household so, among his other duties, he would undertake the record-keeping for the dwelling and educate the children.

Monasteries and convents also played their part in the life of the general populace. They provided food and shelter to travellers and pilgrims, an essential service, as in earlier centuries inns were scarce. They educated the young boys who were destined to enter the priesthood as well as the sons of nobles. Monasteries and convents were charitable institutions, giving food and alms to the poor. In most there would be someone, or a few people, well-versed in herbs and medicines. Also, they provided hospitals for the sick who were brought to the door.

The influence of religion was apparent in the daily lives of all medieval Christians. When they were born they were baptized, they attended mass on Sunday, they were confirmed, married by the priest, took communion, did penance and were buried in holy ground. While, of course, not everyone followed the rules of the Church, the majority did try.

Employment

Although much of the medieval rural population would have been peasants tied to the land, a substantial number of people, especially in towns, were employed in other ways.

In the High and Late Middle Ages, from the eleventh century until the fifteenth century, new towns were being created and existing ones were expanding. With this expansion came trade. Merchants, who once peddled their wares from place to place, often settled in one town and ran their business from there, as did a large number of craftsmen. However, individual tradesmen were at risk of exploitation from whoever owned the land on which the town was built and escalating taxes could be crippling. In a response to this, guilds were formed in most towns.

payments such as the soul-scot, a gift given at funerals, and plow-alms, which were payments made to the Church for every use of a plough between certain dates.

The priest would often be the only educated man in a parish and, as such, would be responsible for record-keeping and the religious education of parishioners. His advice could be sought on other subjects such as morality and legal issues. This said, sometimes in smaller parishes the clergyman in residence would be uneducated and so unable to perform this service. He could also be very poor, as in the more impoverished parishes income would be small and if he was not the holder of the living, the priest would receive just a small proportion of what was paid to the Church by the parishioners.

Guilds were responsible for protecting the interests of their members, making sure that prices were fixed at a certain level and that workmanship was of a good standard. There were two kinds: the merchant guild and the craft guild. The former was for merchants who bought and sold wares and the latter for the craftsmen who made such items as candles, clothes and jewellery.

Guilds would eventually control all aspects of trade in most towns and, by the thirteenth century, the majority of the most powerful men in a town, including the mayor, would be guild members. They regulated all commercial activity and presided over every trader in the town, all of whom had to live by their rules. Outsiders wishing to trade would be charged a fee or even stopped from trading altogether. Anyone who broke guild rules was fined; transgressions included shoddy workmanship and practising a trade without being a member of the guild.

The craft guilds were slightly different from the merchant guilds because there was one guild for each craft rather than one overarching guild covering all craftsmen. There was a large number of different craft guilds because practically every craft had a guild. These included guilds for goldsmiths, dyers, masons, bakers, barbers, saddlers, farriers, vintners and wheelwrights, as well as many others. A woman could become a member of a guild if she was the widow of a guild member and had worked in the craft with him, which she invariably would have done because most craft businesses were family affairs.

These craft guilds regulated aspects such as the price and quality of items produced. They also controlled who joined the guild and who moved up to the next level within the hierarchy. There were three levels within the guild – apprentice, journeyman and master. An apprentice would work with a master for at least five years, sometimes up to nine, learning his craft. He would not be paid, but would have bed, board and clothes provided by the master. Once the apprenticeship was over, the apprentice would become a journeyman, which meant that he could work for a master and earn a wage. If the journeyman could prove a high level of skill, he could eventually rise to the level of master and have his own workshop and apprentices. However, it was very difficult to rise to the level of master in the close community of the guild.

Of course, there were other jobs in the towns and cities as well, but they were not as respectable as those undertaken by the guild members. At the bottom of town society there would be people such as the gravediggers, hangmen, prostitutes, tinkers and rag-sellers.

Outside the towns, there was employment in the castles and manor houses of the nobility as well as on the land. The number of people employed would depend on the size of the dwelling and the wealth of the lord. The richest in the land would employ hundreds of people in a variety of different roles. In a very wealthy household a majordomo or steward would be employed to oversee all of the domestic side of life in the house, and his counterpart looking after the stables was the marshal. Other high-ranking servants were the chamberlain who looked after lord's chambers and the master of the

wardrobe who was responsible for clothing. The high-ranking servants would be assisted by pages, grooms and valets if necessary. Other servants would be employed to do a wide variety of other tasks for the household. These servants could include a cook who, often assisted by scullions, was responsible for preparing the food; a butler who was in charge of the buttery where the drinks such as ale were stored; a herald who would make announcements to the public on behalf of the king or a noble; and a baker who was responsible for baking the bread for the household.

There could also be many people employed outside the manor house. These included, among many others, the blacksmiths who shoed horses and maintained armour; carpenters who made furniture and repaired broken woodwork; and porters who looked after the castle entrance, controlling all who went in and out.

Food in the Middle Ages

The medieval diet varied dramatically depending on class. The nobility had a diverse diet while peasants had to subsist on much sparser fare.

One main staple for all was cereal. The nobility ate wheat, which needed well-fertilized fields to grow, while the poorer peasants ate barley and rye. For the rich, the wheat would be made into white bread called manchet, whereas the poor had instead thick, coarse rye and barley bread.

Pottage was another staple of the medieval diet. It was a soup-stew made from oats or barley and often included vegetables such as peas, beans, cabbage or leeks, and

ABOVE In the Middle Ages, masons were highly skilled workers responsible for building many of the ornate and awe-inspiring churches, cathedrals and castles that can still be seen today.

herbs. The wealthy would eat thick pottage containing meat or fish and a variety of vegetables, herbs and spices. However, the poor would have a thinner version which rarely included meat and was made with vegetables and herbs that they had grown. Most peasants would have a pot of pottage constantly on the fire or in the hot ashes and it was often eaten daily.

Some of the lower classes would have access to fruit, perhaps from an apple or pear tree on their land. Fruit was usually cooked: some believed that raw fruit could make them ill. They would also gather nuts and berries in local forests as vital supplements to their diet.

Some wealthier peasants would have a cow or a few sheep and so had milk, cheese and butter. However, many households had just a few chickens and perhaps a pig for meat because they were cheap to feed and could run free, eating scraps. Although there would have been a number of animals such as deer, boars and hares on local land and in the forests, these belonged to the lord of the manor and to kill one was a punishable offence. Fish was

also sometimes available from rivers or the sea, though rivers were often owned by a lord and permission was needed to fish. Scarcity of meat meant the peasants' diet lacked protein and a number of other vitamins and minerals, which led to ill health.

Peasants were mainly self-sufficient, so when there had been a bad harvest or crops were ruined because of bad weather they went hungry, and the pottage pot would include anything they could find, from acorns to leaves. Sometimes, as happened in northern Europe in the early fourteenth century, bad weather would cause such widespread crop failure that famine would ensue, leading to the deaths of thousands (see pages 61–62).

The diet of the wealthy was very different. They would have an abundance of food with great variety.

They would eat meat and fish with rich sauces and vegetables. A dish that would also often be served was frumenty, a thick pottage which could include meat, milk or eggs and sometimes spices, such as cinnamon or saffron, and sugar. There would be many flavours since herbs and spices would be used along with wine and vinegar. Imported goods such as almonds, dates and figs would also be eaten. Sweets made from fruits from the orchard or woods would be plentiful, as would honey from their bees.

Religion played a very important part in the medieval diet and eating meat was banned on certain days of the week and during Lent. During these times, fish could be eaten instead. The Church also called for days of fasting.

The rich would often drink wine, which would be bought by the barrel and placed in jugs on the table. Their servants, however, drank ale or beer, which were the main drinks for the lower classes because water was often too dirty to drink. Ale was made from water, malt or barley and yeast while beer included hops.

Food preservation was essential, as little food grew in winter. Meat and fish were salted, either by burying them in salt or soaking them in salt water. Before they were eaten, the meat and fish were soaked and rinsed several times to try to remove the salty taste. Fruit, meat and grains were dried by leaving them out in the sun in warm climes. Fish was also smoked to preserve it, as were some meats. Pickling using vinegar or brine was also a favoured method of preservation.

The diet of those in the Mediterranean and Middle East differed somewhat from that of the northern Europeans. However, as in Europe, grains, especially wheat, were dietary staples. Spices and olive oil were much used in cooking. As pork was forbidden by Islam, the main sources of meat were sheep and goats. Sugar was imported from India in the mid-eighth century and became very popular. Also popular were oranges, lemons and other citrus fruits, which provided much needed vitamin C. Sweets made out of ingredients including almonds, dates, honey and sugar were also common. At the start of the Middle Ages wine was still a popular drink. However, with the rise of Islam, tea became the more favoured beverage.

ABOVE Peasants would eat lunch in the fields where they worked. At home, a pot of pottage would often be a permanent fixture above the fire.

BELOW A cannon on a wooden mount, which is on display in the donjon (or keep) of the Château de Loaches. During the Middle Ages, the advent of the cannon led to them gradually replacing siege engines. Their use led to a change in the way fortifications were built with walls being constructed thicker and buildings shorter to withstand cannon attacks.

Science and Technology

During the 1,000 years of the Middle Ages many advances were made in science. It was in the Islamic world that the first scientific developments of the time were made: in the early years, there was seemingly little interest in scientific investigation in the West.

In the Caliphate there was great interest in the scientific discoveries of the ancient world or, more precisely, those of the Greeks. The findings of the great Greek philosophers and scientists, such as Aristotle, Ptolemy and Archimedes, were translated and housed in great libraries. Their theories and findings were then built upon, with great progress being made in the fields of astronomy, alchemy (early chemistry) and mathematics. Arabic numerals were first developed in India during the Early Middle Ages. However, it was the Islamic scientists who were responsible for introducing them to Europe during the High Middle Ages. They also used this system of counting to further develop algebra, a subject in which they made great advances.

In the West it was not until around the twelfth century that interest in scientific study was revitalized. With the crusades and the Reconquista, the West once again was exposed to the learning of the ancient Greeks and some of the Islamic developments. This led to ancient works being translated into Latin and thus being accessible to those in the Western world. Over the next few centuries many advances were made in a number of different fields, such as optics and kinetics. Many of the great medieval universities were founded around this period, further fuelling scientific discovery and teaching.

In the field of technology the Middle Ages was a time of great invention. There were innovations in just about every field, from farming to architecture and from warmongering to timekeeping. The significance of these inventions is illustrated by the fact that many of them are still in use today in one form or another.

Below are listed some of the significant inventions of the Middle Ages:

Blast Furnaces – these first appeared in the West in Switzerland in the High Middle Ages and were used for the smelting process to produce much larger quantities of iron than had been possible before.

Cannon – developed in China, cannon were first used in western Europe during the High Middle Ages.

Eyeglasses – developed in the late thirteenth century, eyeglasses were initially only for the long-sighted.

Full Plate Armour – although plate iron armour

BELOW A brass
astrolabe from
Saragossa, dating
from c. 1079–1080.
Although the
astrolabe had been
used in fields such as
navigation, astrology
and astronomy since
ancient times, it
seems only to have
started to be used
widely during the
Middle Ages when
many advance-
ments were made
to the design.

was developed throughout the later Middle Ages from around the thirteenth century, the full suit of plate armour did not appear until the start of the fifteenth century. These suits of armour gave the wearers protection while still allowing them freedom of movement.

Gutenberg Printing Press – perhaps the most important invention of them all, the invention of the Gutenberg printing press made the spread of information easier and paved the way for the written word to be brought to the masses (see page 97).

Horseshoe – although there is some mention of horseshoes in ancient texts, the nailed-on shoe seems to have been invented in the Early Middle Ages, allowing horses to carry heavy loads over rough terrain.

Horse collar – invented in the ninth century, the horse collar made the horse a much more effective draught animal.

Hour glass – it is not known exactly when in the Middle Ages the hour glass came into use, but by the Late Middle Ages it was in common use as a reliable, inexpensive way to tell the time.

Longbow – developed around the twelfth century, the longbow became the deciding factor in many of the battles fought by the English, especially during the Hundred Years' War. In skilled hands the accuracy, rate of fire and range achieved by the longbow far surpassed those achieved by other bows.

Magnetic compass – the magnetic compass came into use in Europe around the twelfth century and aided navigation considerably, especially in poor visibility.

Mechanical clock – this time-telling device was invented in the Late Middle Ages and became a familiar sight in clock towers around Europe.

Spinning wheel – probably originating in the East, the spinning wheel revolutionized the manufacture of yarn in Europe from the High Middle Ages.

Wheelbarrow – this late twelfth-century invention made many jobs in construction and farming easier.

Windmill – invented in the High Middle Ages, the vertical windmill made the grinding of grain a much more efficient affair.

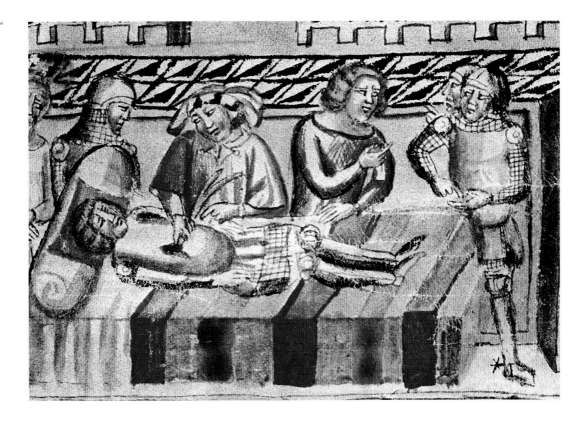

Medicine

During the Middle Ages there was no knowledge of germs and little understanding of what caused the spread of infection. Sickness was blamed on many diverse things, from sin to the planets being out of alignment. Therefore, when diseases such as the plague took hold, especially in the cramped and unsanitary living condition of medieval towns, they would spread like wildfire.

Lack of hygiene and their poor diet meant that the lower classes were very susceptible to illness and the rich did not fare that much better. Folk remedies based on herbs and other ingredients were often used as cures. For the poor these could be provided by a wise woman in the village, whereas the wealthy would be able to afford a physician to attend to them.

Surgery, including the pulling of teeth, was often performed by barbers. It was unlikely that the instruments used would be sterilized because there was little understanding of the importance of hygiene. This meant that many patients died from infection after surgery. In the Middle Ages it seems that you were often just as likely to die from the treatment as the illness.

Although at the start of the Middle Ages there was little understanding of anatomy and the cause of disease, there were many advancements in medicine during the period. One of the greatest influences on medical theory was the Greek physician, Galen of Pergamum. Although he had been dead for more than two centuries by the start of the Middle Ages, his writings still existed. They were translated, mainly into Arabic, around the ninth century and into Latin by western scholars around the eleventh century. These works were then used to teach medicine in both the east and the west.

Galen believed that there were four "humours" in the body – blood, phlegm, black bile and yellow bile – and that it was when these were unbalanced that a person became ill. Medieval physicians would redress the balance using a number of methods. Perhaps the most famous of these was bloodletting. Leeches were attached to the body to release the excess blood that physicians believed was contained in patients with a high fever and other illnesses.

In the Islamic world the study of medicine was very highly regarded. A number of Islamic physicians who had studied, taught and practised medicine wrote medical texts. One of these was Abu al-Qasim, possibly the greatest Islamic physician of the age. He wrote a comprehensive 30-part medical treatise that was used for almost 500 years. His work not only incorporated the thinking of past experts, but also contained new material and many drawings, including some of surgical devices he had invented.

Not only did the Islamic world provide a number of great physicians, but also some brilliant pharmacists as well. Alchemists came across many substances during their experiments and many of these were found to have medicinal benefits. From these they developed a variety of drugs which were successfully used by the physicians, some for many centuries. They are even thought to have used parts of the poppy to help relieve pain, a treatment that is still in use to this day, using a different formula, in the form of morphine.

In the West schools of medicine were established. The first of these was founded in Salerno, Italy, during the ninth century. It achieved greatness during the

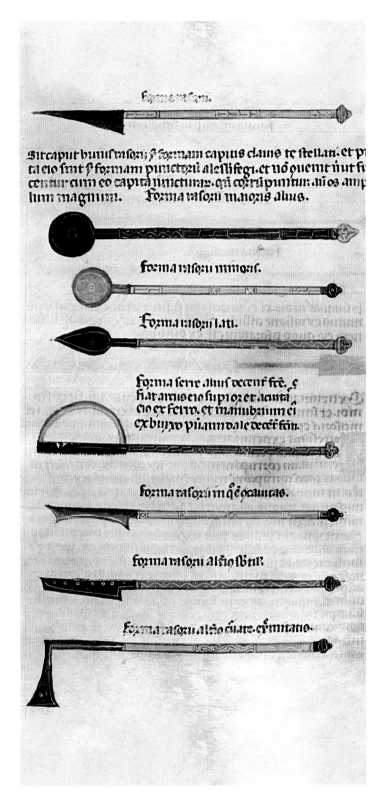

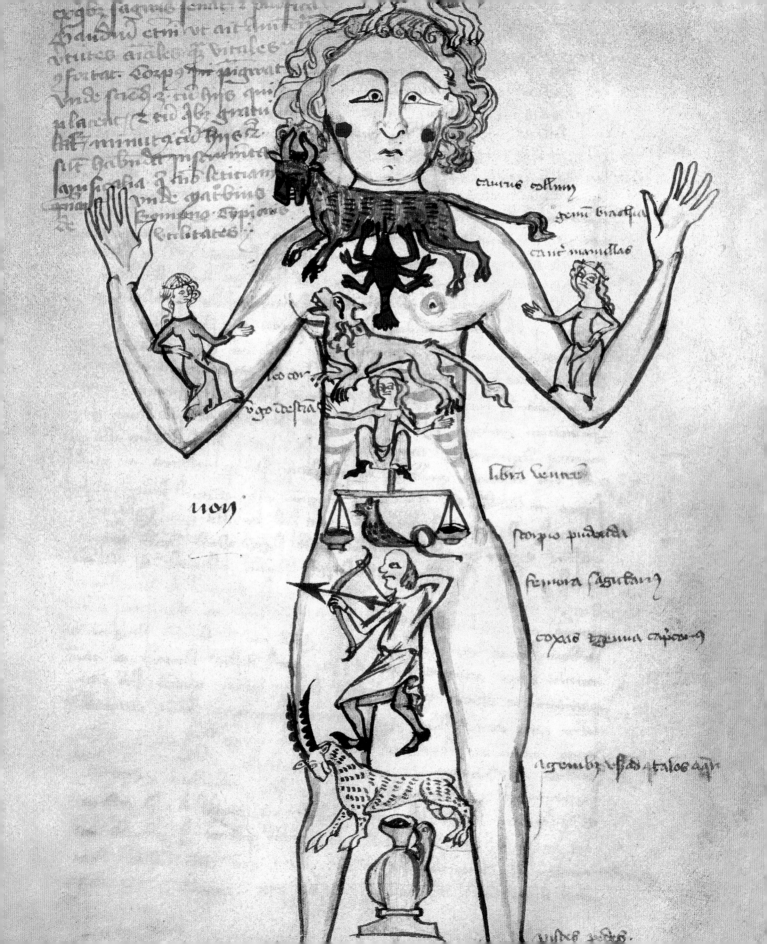

High Middle Ages. Salerno was followed with schools in Paris and Montpellier in France and in Padua and Bologna in Italy. These seats of learning helped to spread advancements in medicine throughout western Europe. Around the fourteenth century dissections were increasing in popularity and the first anatomy text was published in 1316 by Mondino de Liuzzi, an Italian anatomist. Though not wholly accurate, this text was used by physicians for the next 200 years.

During the Middle Ages hospitals for treating the sick and were established throughout Europe and beyond. In Europe, these were often part of religious institutions such as monasteries. The monks and nuns would nurse the patients and look after their spiritual wellbeing. In the Islamic world hospitals were founded in 0many of the great cities such as Damascus and Baghdad.

These were remarkable because it is believed that they treated anyone, no matter what their race or creed.

Though it would be many years before human anatomy and the cause and spread of infection would be fully understood, the contribution made to medicine by the physicians and scientists of the Middle Ages should not be overlooked, as their work was the starting point for the discoveries that were to come.

The Crises of the Fourteenth Century

The fourteenth century was, perhaps, one of the darkest times of the Middle Ages. Seemingly everything that could be wrong with the world was wrong – war, pestilence, poverty, hunger, discontent, revolution and religious discord all played their part in the downturn of Europe's fortunes.

The manuscript text within the image (Old French, part of the illustration):

E nfuere aleient chascū ior
Ⓜ estier lor en ert ⁊ besoing
Ⓜ out lor cōuent agētreloing
2 i filz le roi furent ploze
2 nor qui furent enterre

G arqeus orcut troi
S iles mistrēt enz ai
ẅ eles leur frere ba
E ntcerre furent n

J lpzis furēt ⁊ euseloz

A la plꝰ belle tell
S onz ael na cuer c

ABOVE Scenes showing the disposal of victims of the Plague, from a 14th-century manuscript. The plague seemed to strike every corner of Europe killing people in their thousands. Due to the terrible extent of the disease a vast number of bodies needed to be disposed of. That meant that proper, individual burials were often replaced with the use of mass graves and cremations.

OPPOSITE A monk bleeding a patient, from the Luttrell Psalter, which was begun before 1340.

The start of the century was plagued by bad weather which heralded the start of what has been dubbed the "Little Ice Age". Long, cruel winters and wet, cold summers led to ruined harvests. The year 1315 was a terrible one. Crops failed throughout northern Europe and the price of food shot to unprecedented levels. The following year delivered more of the same and 1317 was worse still. Population growth at the end of the preceding century meant that in a good year just enough food could be produced to feed the population. Therefore, by 1317, food stores were all but used up and the poor could not afford to eat. People survived on what they could forage, even eating bark from the trees and draught animals. Although the weather improved in the summer of 1317, many people were so weak that they were susceptible to disease and often succumbed to illnesses that, in better times, they would have had a chance of fighting off. Much of the grain needed to plant the next season's food had been eaten so, even though the weather improved, it would be almost a decade before the food supply recovered. Though the exact level of mortality caused by the Great Famine can only be guessed at, it is thought that at least ten per cent of the population of the affected area died.

Just as Europe was recovering from the Great Famine, it was to be hit by an even worse crisis. Gradually creeping west from its origins in central Asia, a terrible disease was making its way overland to Europe, killing many as it went. Eventually, it became waterborne and, probably hitching a ride on Genoese ships from the Crimea, it reached the Mediterranean in 1347. From there it sped west across Europe and south into the Holy Land and Africa, following trade routes. It seemed that nowhere was to be spared as it reached the most remote settlements such as those on Greenland, the Shetlands and Iceland. It is thought that this terrible plague, which is sometimes known as the Black Death, wiped out a third of the world's population, with some cities losing up to 60 per cent of their inhabitants, in main because of their cramped, unhygienic living conditions.

There were many far-reaching consequences of the Black Death, not least the death of many workers both skilled and unskilled. However, there was one particularly disturbing consequence that was a result, not of the disease itself, but of ignorance and greed. Although many Jews died of the Black Death, rumours spread across Europe that they were responsible for the pestilence by poisoning wells. Despite the pope and other rulers disavowing such claims, the rumours resulted in dire consequences for Jews, especially those in Germany and Switzerland. In Strasbourg the Jewish population, except those who converted to Christianity, was rounded up and burned to death. This tragic scene was replayed again and again across northern Europe, with many Jewish communities being completely exterminated. As Jewish property was often confiscated and any debts that they held cancelled, it can only be assumed that greed played no small part in the fate of the Jews.

The Black Death had a huge impact on Europe and, for some, out of the ashes rose a new world of opportunity. The death of many workers meant that labourers were now in demand. This gave them the leeway to ask for higher wages and opportunities that they would not have had before. For example, craft guilds, which before the Plague had often recruited from the same families, out of necessity threw the net wider for apprentices, giving others a chance to have a trade. However, having barely glimpsed the improved living conditions that might be theirs, the peasantry found the door to opportunity slammed in their faces. Governments in western Europe were quick to react to stamp on any opportunism. Wage caps were introduced and legislation was enacted to prevent much progress. For example, in England in 1351 the Statute of Labourers banned wage increases and stopped labourers from moving away from their homes, in effect stopping them from taking advantage of the labour shortages to improve their lives. These laws were to have far-reaching consequences across the continent for decades.

France fared particularly badly during the first half of the fourteenth century. Not only did the population suffer during the Great Famine and the plague epidemic, but their country was ravaged by the Hundred Years' War (see pages 146–147), which had resulted in widespread death and destruction. Nor was that all the peasants of France had to deal with. In 1356 King John II had been captured at the Battle of Poitiers, which was just one of a string of defeats that combined to make the peasants lose faith in, and respect for, the nobles. Added to that, the nobility increased taxes and, by order of the dauphin, the future Charles V, forced the peasants to work on repairing their castles for nothing. It is not surprising

then that some peasants had had enough. On 21 May 1358 in the Oise valley in northern France an uprising, that was to become known as the Jacquerie, began.

The uprising spread quickly and the peasants destroyed castles, sacked towns and were responsible for the murders of many nobles and their families, some in truly horrific ways. The uprising was finally put down by Charles the Bad of Navarre, the son-in-law of King John II, at the Battle of Mello on 10 June 1358. The victory was followed by the massacre of thousands of the rebels, with reprisals against the insurgents continuing long after the revolt was over. For the deaths of perhaps a few hundred nobles, it is estimated that around 20,000 peasants lost their lives.

In England discontent was also rife among the peasantry. Although they were aggrieved by the 1351 Statute of Labourers, it was not until three decades after the statute was enacted that the sense of grievance would violently explode. The final straw was the levying of the 1381 poll tax – a per capita tax – the third in four years. It wasn't just the tax being levied that angered the populace, but also that the people were expected to pay three times as much as had been required in 1377 and 1379.

In May 1381 rebellion broke out and in early June, rebels from Kent and Essex marched on London. The Kentish rebels were led by perhaps the most famous figure of the uprising, Wat Tyler. Once in London, the Kentish rebels took the Tower of London and executed Archbishop Simon of Sudbury and Sir Robert Hales, the treasurer, both of whom they held responsible for the poll tax. They also destroyed the palace of the king's extremely unpopular uncle, John of Gaunt. The Essex rebels, meanwhile, met the young King Richard II at Mile End outside London. Richard made them a number of promises, including the abolition of forced labour, fair trade and fairer rent.

The main aim of the actions of the rebels in London was seemingly to force the king to negotiate and make concessions. In that it appeared to have succeeded, as Richard met Wat Tyler and the Kentish rebels at Smithfield on 15 June. However, Wat Tyler was attacked and wounded during the discussions. Although taken to St Bartholomew's hospital, he was then dragged from there and beheaded on the orders of the Lord Mayor of London, Sir William Walworth. The king managed to calm the enraged rebels and they dispersed. Richard reneged on his promises and the rebellion was thoroughly put down in the following weeks and many of the leaders were executed. It had taken less than a month to put down the rebellion with the rebels achieving very little, apart from demonstrating the dissatisfaction of the people.

The Jacquerie and the English Peasants' Revolt were just two of a number of peasant revolts that took place across Europe in the fourteenth and fifteenth centuries. In most cases the peasants were no match for the governing classes and the uprisings did not end well for most of those involved.

CHAPTER

3

"THE EYE THROUGH
WHICH I SEE GOD IS
THE SAME EYE THROUGH
WHICH GOD SEES ME;
MY EYE AND GOD'S
EYE ARE ONE EYE, ONE
SEEING, ONE KNOWING,
ONE LOVE."

MEISTER ECKHART (c. 1260–c. 1328)

...odem die incipio mona... / ...liciano, com...ienda...r...

no uibente papa tria uitrib' / deo et beato Petro eiusq; ui

nf cancellis sacrauint alta / rus. romanis scilicet pontif

. Tunc papa uir sacndo nuf / Quox numero uel ordini di

q; agendo. p alia salutis hor / me dignatio licet indignum

nta. coram epis & cardinalibus / sociauit: me olim monachu

ultox q; psonis. huicemodi / priorem q; monasterii huuif

...be... habuit ad pplin. / domno ac uenerabili hugon

RELIGION

Pope Gregory and the Rise of the Papacy

Pope Gregory I played perhaps the most significant role in the rise of the papacy and the continual spread of Christianity throughout Europe in the Early Middle Ages.

He had political astuteness and a true devotion to those less fortunate, which made for a formidable combination. He was voted in as pope in 590, though he had never sought the office, preferring life as a monk. It was a difficult time to be pope because Italy had been ravaged by war and was now ruled by the Arian Christian Lombards in the north and the Roman Catholic Byzantines in the south. Rome had been neglected by the Byzantines who protected Ravenna at all costs, leaving Rome vulnerable to the Lombards, who were a huge threat. Gregory was left very much in charge of Rome because the Emperor Maurice was occupied with fighting the Persians, Slavs and Avars and seemed to care little for the fate of the city. It was Gregory who had to stop the Lombards from sacking Rome and pay them to stay away. He also sought to facilitate peace in Italy through diplomacy and he was, in some part, successful.

Gregory was also, among other things, a diplomat, treasurer and supporter of the poor. As there was no support from the emperor, he organized the church funds so that they were directed towards the relief of the needy, many of whom were refugees from the Lombard lands. He used his own and church lands to produce food which was given away to the people of Rome, who had been brought to the brink of starvation by war. As a result of his good deeds, it was to Gregory that the people looked for leadership, cementing the influence of the papacy in the ruling of Italy for centuries to come.

Gregory also sought to further the teachings of the Church and to bring papal authority to Roman Catholics throughout Europe, no mean feat in a continent ruled by many different tribes and riven by conflict. He sent a mission of 40 monks under Saint Augustine to England in 597 to convert the pagan Anglo-Saxon tribes to Christianity. It was a success and Gregory founded a cathedral in Canterbury. Other missions were then sent out from England to spread the Roman Catholic faith in mainland western Europe. It was the start of a slow spread of Roman Catholicism throughout the continent, which culminated in a transformed Europe that by the Late Middle Ages was completely under the influence of the Church.

The Rule of Saint Benedict

Gregory I was a prolific writer and many of his writings survive. In Book II of his *Dialogues*, Gregory tells of a holy man called Benedict of Nursia. As a young man Benedict was sent to Rome to study. However, once there, he found himself becoming disillusioned with the dissolute behaviour of his peers. This led to him leaving Rome and

RIGHT Pope
Gregory I is
depicted writing
his *Dialogues* (or
Lives of the Saints)
with the help of
four disciples of
Saint Benedict.

OPPOSITE Saint
Benedict was
revered during his
life as a good and
holy man. He is
the patron saint
of Europe. Here
he exorcises a
possessed monk.

the conduct he found so disturbing. He first moved to Enfide (now known as Affile) and then to a hillside cave in the Abruzzi region some 64 kilometres (40 miles) to the east of Rome. He lived alone in his cave, by a lake, for three years. Romanus, a monk from one of the many nearby monasteries, brought him food and clothing.

Benedict gained the respect of those around him for his holiness and purity of spirit. Thus, when the abbot of one of the local monasteries died, Benedict was asked to take his place. However, this move was not a success and when Benedict's reformations led to the monks trying to poison

him, he returned to his cave. His reputation was such though that many people came to be guided by him. This led to him building 12 monasteries, each populated with a superior and 12 monks and all overseen by Benedict himself. When Benedict left the area, his monasteries continued, taking novices and providing education. Benedict's final home was at Monte Cassino, where he founded a monastery on the site of a temple of Apollo in around 529; it was here that he wrote his famous Rule.

The *Rule of Saint Benedict* (*Regula Benedicti*) was the directory laid down by Benedict to govern the

LEFT Henry IV
(1050–1106) was
the Holy Roman
Emperor of
Germany from 1056.
Excommunicated
twice by Pope
Gregory VII, he is
shown waiting for
an audience with the
Pope at Canossa.

running of a monastery and the daily lives of those who resided within its walls. There is no evidence that Benedict intended to found a monastic order. His *Rule* was aimed at autonomous communities, making them self-sufficient and self-governing; more of a family than a cold institution. The abbot, who was elected for life and answerable only to God, ran the monastery and was responsible for the souls of every monk in his monastery. This father figure controlled all goings-on from the appointment of officials to the organization of daily life. All the "brother" monks who lived under the abbot's rule had their day organized into a strict timetable of prayer and work. They had to give up their worldly possessions and take vows of chastity, poverty and obedience. As this kind of life was not for everyone, Benedict introduced a probationary year to weed out those who were not suited to the life. With the aim being not a life of privation for its members, but a harmonious community working and worshipping together, the *Rule of Saint Benedict* is still one most commonly used by monasteries today and Benedict has become known as "the father of Western monasticism".

Christianity in the Eleventh Century

The eleventh century saw great changes to the Church. Up to the middle of the eleventh century, there were already disputes between the Byzantine Imperial Church in the east and the Latin Church in the west over doctrine and spiritual matters.

However, it was not until 1054 that these differences were to cause a permanent division between the two. The eastern Church refused to accept the supremacy of the pope and concede to the dictates of the Latin Church. This led Pope Leo IX to excommunicate Patriarch Michael Cerularius, the head of the eastern Church. Celrularius retaliated by excommunicating the pope. These actions caused the Great Schism, a permanent division between the two Churches, which eventually gave us the Greek Orthodox and Roman Catholic Churches that can be seen today.

The Great Schism was not the only significant event to affect the Church in the eleventh century. Towards the end of the century another hugely significant conflict was taking place. The Investiture Controversy started when Pope Gregory VII challenged the right of the German

King Henry IV to appoint bishops. Although bishops were supposed to be invested by the Church, in reality it was the state that undertook this role. Investiture also brought money into the royal coffers because there were occasions when bishoprics were sold. It also meant that the high-ranking clergy were loyal to the ruler and would, in turn, appoint other loyal clergy.

This lay investiture of the bishops had taken place for many years without opposition from the Church. However, Gregory had decided to instigate a series of reforms designed to give supreme power over the secular states, states that were not ruled by the Church or any other religious body, to the Church. These reforms were laid out in the 1075 *Dictatus papae,* a document containing details of powers assumed by the pope as God's representative on earth, which included the sole right to depose an emperor or appoint clergy.

The removal of lay investiture was partly in response to the prevalence of simony – the selling of holy offices – in the secular state and it was this that led to the Investiture Controversy. In response to the *Dictatus papae,* Henry IV sent Gregory a letter in which he called him a "false monk" and called for the election of a new pope. Gregory, in turn, excommunicated Henry and deposed him. The German nobles used Gregory's actions as an excuse for rebellion and seized royal land. Henry, realizing that he was in the weaker position, met the pope at Canossa in Tuscany in 1077 and begged forgiveness. This was given and the excommunication was lifted. Despite this, Henry was excommunicated and deposed again in 1080, when Gregory supported Rudolf Rheinfeld, a rival for Henry's throne. After Rudolf's death, Henry invaded Italy and attacked Rome. Civil war broke out and Gregory was forced to flee with Norman

protectors. Henry was crowned Holy Roman Emperor in 1084 by Pope Clement III, whom he had chosen as Gregory's replacement. Gregory died soon after.

The Investiture Controversy did not end with Gregory's death, but continued into the twelfth century. Finally, in 1122, a compromise was reached with the Concordat of Worms agreement giving the Church more powers over investiture.

Monastic Reform

The tenth and eleventh centuries saw a number of monastic reforms. The first of these were the Cluniac reforms, which were instigated in an attempt to stem Church corruption. Since monasteries were built on land belonging to the lord of the area, the lord could interfere in Church affairs, which led to offences such as simony. Cluny Abbey was founded in 910 as an attempt to remove this secular influence on the Church. Its founder, William I, Duke of Aquitaine, had the abbey built on his

land and then placed it under the direct control of the pope with the only obligation to William being that of prayer. This Benedictine monastery, rather than existing independently from other monasteries, was the first of a great number of monasteries, all of which came under the overall control of the Abbot of Cluny. Throughout the eleventh century the Cluniac movement rapidly grew so that, by the end of the century, there were more than 1,000 Cluny monasteries.

In 1098 there was to be further monastic reform. A group of about 20 monks, who wished to live a more devout life than was possible at their monastery in Molesme in Burgundy, left the monastery and established their own community at a place called Citeaux, south of Dijon. The Cistercian order took its name from Cistercium, the Latin for Citeaux. There they followed the Benedictine rule in its earliest form and rejected all later changes to the rule. They placed great emphasis on manual labour and austerity. By the fifteenth century, at the height of the order, there were more than 700 Cistercian communities across western Europe.

Papacy in the Late Middle Ages

The discord between the papacy and the secular state, although officially concluded in 1122, still carried on throughout the twelfth century. During his time as pope, from 1198 to 1216, Pope Innocent III was responsible for reasserting and extending papal power, his aim being to cement the papacy as the ultimate authority.

He restored the authority of the pope over the Papal States by taking advantage of internal strife in the Holy Roman Empire. He also involved himself in the politics of other European states, skilfully gaining power for the papacy out of secular conflict. By his death in 1216 he had cemented the authority of the pope and left the groundwork for future popes to build on.

The popes who came after Innocent III during the thirteenth century followed Innocent's example and extended papal authority even further. However, that would change during Boniface VIII's time as pope. At the end of the thirteenth century Edward I of England was at war with Philip IV of France over English holdings in France. Both sides were to some extent funding the war by taxing the clergy. Papal consent was necessary for any secular taxation of the clergy and Boniface

RIGHT The compilation of 27 statements about the powers of the Pope created under the rule of Pope Gregory VII in 1075 (see Transations, page 160).

Dictatus papae.

i Qd Romana eccia a solo dno sit fundata.

ii Qd solus Romanus pontifex iure dicat universalis.

iii Qd ille solus possit deponere epos uel reconciliare.

iiii Qd legatus eius omnibus epis presit in concilio etiam inferioris gradus.
et aduersus eos sententiam depositionis possit dare.

v Qd absentes papa possit deponere.

vi Qd cum excommunicatis ab illo inter cetera nec in eadem domo debemus manere.

vii Qd illi soli liceat pro temporis necessitate nouas leges condere.
nouas plebes congregare. de canonica abbatiam facere. et econtra. diuitem episcopatum diuidere. et inopes unire.

viii Qd solus possit uti imperialibus insignis.

viiii Qd solius papae pedes omnes principes deosculentur.

x Qd illius solius nomen in ecclesiis recitetur.

xi Qd hoc unicum est nomen in mundo.

xii Qd illi liceat imperatores deponere.

xiii Qd illi liceat de sede ad sedem necessitate cogente epos transmutare.

xiiii Qd de omni ecclesia quocumque uoluerit clericum ualeat ordinare.

xv Qd ab illo ordinatus alius ecclesie preesse potest sed non militare. et quod ab aliquo epo non debet superiorem gradum accipere.

xvi Qd nulla synodus absque preccepto eius debet generalis uocari.

xvii Qd nullum capitulum nullusque liber canonicus habeatur absque illius auctoritate.

xviii Qd sententia illius a nullo debeat retractari. et ipse omnium solus retractare possit.

xviiii Qd a nemine ipse iudicari debeat.

xx Qd nullus audeat condemnare apostolicam sedem appellante.

xxi Qd maiores cause cuiuscunque ecclesie ad eam referri debeant.

xxii Qd Romana ecclesia nunquam errauit nec in perpetuum scriptura testante errabit.

xxiii Qd Romanus pontifex si canonice fuerit ordinatus meritis beati Petri indubitanter efficitur sanctus testante sancto synodo papiensi epo cum multis sanctis patribus fauentibus sicut in decretis beati Symmachi papae continetur.

xxiiii Qd illius precepto et licentia subiectis liceat accusare.

xxv Qd absque synodali conuentu possit epos deponere et reconciliare.

xxvi Qd catholicus non habeatur qui non concordat Romane ecclesie.

xxvii Qd a fidelitate iniquorum subiectos potest absoluere.

OPPOSITE An
extract from the *Tres
Riches Heures du
Duch de Berry* – this
book of prayers
was created by the
Limbourg brothers
for John, Duke of
Berry and is believed
to be the best
example of French
Gothic illuminated
manuscripts that
still survives.

RIGHT An
illumination from
1409 showing the
city of Avignon
with a view of
the papal palace.
The "Babylonian
Captivity" was the
period of almost
seven decades when
the papacy resided
in Avignon rather
than Rome. Avignon
was chosen as it
belonged to papal
vassals and because
it was in France.

refused to allow the situation to continue. He issued a bull stating that any taxation of the clergy without papal consent would result in excommunication. In France this declaration did not have the desired effect. Boniface was forced to backtrack, in no small part because of Philip, who retaliated by banning the export of money from France, causing papal revenues to fall. The feud between Philip and Boniface continued, reaching a head in 1302 when Boniface issued the bull *Unam sanctam*. This declared that kings were subordinate to the pope. Philip's response was to have Boniface declared a heretic, among other things, and taken into captivity. During his short captivity Boniface was probably ill-treated and he died soon after his release.

In 1309 the papacy under the French pope Clement V, feeling insecure in Rome because of conflicts between the various power-holding families and under more and more pressure to move from Philip IV, decided to transfer its seat of power. Avignon was chosen as the new papal capital since it was held by papal vassals. The papacy was to remain in Avignon, under the influence of the French crown, for 68 years. All of the Avignon popes were French. During their time at Avignon some popes and cardinals allegedly lived a lavish lifestyle, causing resentment and damaging the reputation of the papacy.

In 1375 a revolt in the Papal States was instigated by Florence, which was concerned about papal territorial expansion, among other things. The war was prosecuted by an eight-member committee called the Eight Saints. The Florentines were excommunicated and other penalties were effected against them. However, they remained defiant. Finally in 1377 Pope Gregory XI dispatched an army to deal with them while he returned to Rome to secure the threatened papal land. The war, which was known as the War of Eight Saints, was finally ended with the Treaty of Tripoli in 1378.

Gregory XI died shortly after returning to Rome and an Italian pope, Urban VI, was elected in his place. However, very early in his reign he managed to alienate a number of cardinals. These cardinals, who were for the most part French, returned to Avignon and elected their own pope. Thus there were two popes, each with an official seat of power and their own cardinals. Each pope had his own supporters, usually drawn along national lines, and excommunicated the supporters of the other pope.

Confusion reigned as the populace of Europe was split between two different views. This state of affairs resulted in a disastrous loss of status for the papacy whose authority inevitably waned. Despite the negative impact of the dual papacy, it was not until 1417 that this "Western Schism" was healed and the papal office was once again restored to a single pope.

John Wycliffe and the Lollards

The Avignon papacy was renowned for its dissipation. John Wycliffe, a fourteenth-century English reformer and dissident, condemned Church excess and called for reform. Believing that the Church should not be rich, he was also opposed to such doctrines as transubstantiation. He wrote and preached extensively about his beliefs during his lifetime and followers of his views formed the Lollard movement around 1382. Wycliffe was accused of heresy, but action was never taken against him. He died in 1384, still preaching his reformist views. Even after his death Wycliffe's influence carried on. The Lollard movement continued, despite brutal repression, into the sixteenth century. Wycliffe is perhaps most famous for instigating the translation of the Bible into English, thus making it accessible to the many who could not understand Latin.

The Rise of Islam

While the papacy was increasing the influence of Christianity in western Europe, south of the continent a new religion was being born. Around the year 610, a merchant from Mecca, in Arabia (now Saudi Arabia), began receiving visions and messages from God.

He went on to preach about these revelations to his family, then to his friends and, finally, to the general populace. The merchant's name was Muhammad and he was the founder of the Islamic faith. He is considered by most Muslims to be the last prophet of God.

Early converts to the Islamic faith were some of Muhammad's family and a number of his friends. However, there was much opposition to this new movement. At that time, the Ka'aba in Mecca was a shrine and a site of pagan pilgrimage and members of the Arab tribes came there to worship the idols that resided within. Many Meccans were concerned that, if their religions were supplanted by a new monotheistic one that did not include idolatry, the commerce coming to Mecca with the pilgrimages would die out. Therefore, it was detrimental to the interests of the rulers and merchants of Mecca to support the new faith of Islam. Muhammad and his followers were victimized and persecuted. Muhammad himself was a member of the prominent Banu Hashim clan, which was led by his uncle, Abu Talib, and he had the protection of the clan. This meant that he was reasonably safe from physical attack, but not all of his followers were so lucky and some were attacked or killed.

Muhammad's life changed dramatically in the year 619. It was a time of great sadness for him because both his loyal wife of 25 years and Abu Talib died. Not only was he left without two of the most important people in his life, he was now also without the protection of the clan because the new leader did not support him. This left him in a perilous situation: without protection, he was open to attack from his enemies. Muhammad and his followers needed a new, safer home. Muhammad

ABOVE The courtyard
of the Ummayad
Mosque, Damascus,
Syria.

OPPOSITE The
Great Mosque of
Damascus was built
by the Umayyad
Caliph al-Walid
I. It is the oldest
stone-built mosque
to still exist today
and is home to a
shrine that is said to
contain the head of
St John the Baptist.

started negotiations with a delegation from the city of
Yathrib (now known as Medina) and, following a pledge
of protection from its citizens, he and his followers
migrated there in 622.

In Medina Muhammed and his followers were made
welcome and many of the citizens converted to Islam.
Muhammad became both a political and religious leader
and saw his power grow. There was still bad feeling
between the followers of Muhammed and the Meccans
who had persecuted them. The property of the Muslims
in Mecca had been seized by the Meccans and, in return,
the Muslims raided Meccan caravans, regaining their
lost wealth. The situation came to a head in 624, when
300 Muslim soldiers met a Meccan force numbering
1,000 men at Badr, about 130 kilometres (80 miles) from
Medina. The battle resulted in defeat for the Meccans
and reinforced Muhammad's position in Medina,

making him even more powerful than before. Badr was
the first major battle fought by the Muslims and it is of
great importance because it can be considered to be the
start of the militarized spread of Islam and centuries of
Muslim expansion.

Badr did not end the conflict with Mecca and more
skirmishes and battles followed over the next few years.
The Muslims lost the next major battle against the
Meccans. However, in 627 they were again victorious
when Medina was besieged by the Meccans. In 628, a
truce was agreed with Mecca. The peace was not to last,
though, and when the truce was broken by the Meccans,
Muhammad marched on Mecca and took control of the
city. His first act on entering the city was to order the
removal of all the idols from the Ka'aba. It was then
rededicated as an Islamic place of worship because
it was built on the foundations of a shrine built by

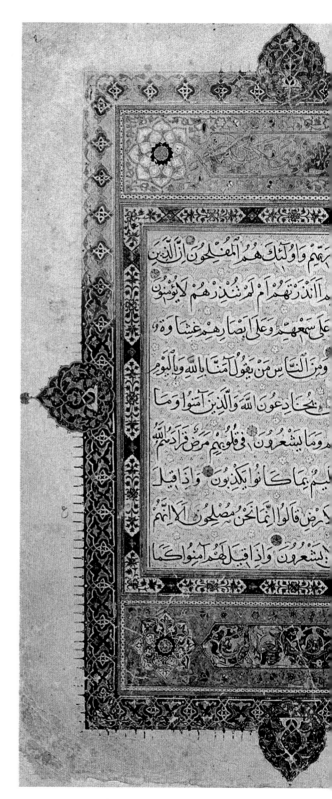

Abraham, one of the most important figures common to the three major religions of Islam, Christianity and Judaism. It became the most sacred site in Islam, and though pilgrimages still took place to Mecca, they were now a Muslim rite.

Islam was by that time slowly spreading throughout Arabia. A few years before his death, Muhammad led an army into northern Arabia, towards Syria, making alliances and conquests along the way. Through Muhammad's treaties with various nomadic tribes, Islam was spread still further and by 632 much of Arabia was Islamic. In that year, Muhammad made the first truly Islamic pilgrimage to the Ka'aba at Mecca, after which he gave his final sermon at Mount Arafat, to the east of the city. He died a few months later in Medina, where he was buried. His tomb is part of the Mosque of the Prophet and today sits under a striking green dome.

When Muhammad died, he was succeeded by his close friend and adviser, Abu Bakr, who became the first caliph, or "successor", and the first caliph of the Rashidun Caliphate. The Caliphate was the Muslim state ruled by a caliph which was established after the death of Muhammad. Abu Bakr began the Muslim conquests by invading both the Persian and Byzantine Empires. As these two great realms had been almost continuously at war with each other for the best part of a century, both were weak and not capable of mounting an effective defence. The Persian Sassanid Empire was the first to be targeted: in 633 Abu Bakr invaded Iraq, the wealthiest part of the Empire. Once Iraq was conquered, the invasion of the eastern territory of the Byzantine Empire commenced and the Muslim army marched on Byzantine Syria from Iraq. The Muslims were battling two great empires simultaneously. Despite this, when Abu Bakr died in 634 Muslim forces were already besieging the great city of Damascus.

Abu Bakr was succeeded by the caliph Umar, who oversaw an even more rapid expansion of Islamic territory. His rule was marked by his diplomatic skill and his treatment of conquered people. He allowed them to keep their non-Muslim religions and property and gave them protection in return for a tax called *jizya* and their acceptance of Muslim rule. Umar was followed by two more Rashidun caliphs. By the time Ali, Muhammad's

cousin and the final Rashidun caliph, died in 661 almost all of the Middle East and the whole of Persia were under Islamic rule.

Civil war ended the Rashidun Caliphate and, after the death of Ali, the new Umayyad Caliphate was established. The Umayyads made Damascus the capital of the Islamic world and in 715 building of the Great Mosque was completed there. Under the Umayyads, Islamic territory continued to increase. The expansion into Byzantine lands continued until, in 674, the Muslim force reached Constantinople and besieged it for the first time. In 678 they were defeated and they did not return to attack Constantinople again for another 30 years, when they were soundly defeated again. However, they still occupied former Byzantine lands up to Antioch and the Antolian plateau.

North Africa was totally subjugated by 709, so the caliphate turned its attention to Hispania (present-day Spain and Portugal). The destruction of the Visigoth Empire ensued and the Muslims occupied the Iberian Peninsula as far north as Asturias. They would have conquered further had they not been forced back by the Franks in south France in 732. During the Umayyad Caliphate, the Muslim state reached its greatest extent and the Byzantine Empire had been reduced to a fifth of its original size. In 750, the Umayyad dynasty was overthrown by the Abbasids and a new caliphate was founded. Only one Umayyad prince survived the massacre of the Umayyads by the Abbasids. He founded the autonomous Emirate of Cordoba in the Iberian Peninsula, which was to flourish over the next few centuries.

The Abassid Caliphate ruled until the sixteenth century. One of the first changes they made was to move the capital from Damascus to Iraq, where they founded the city of Baghdad in 762. They also delegated much of the authority of the caliph to local rulers, called emirs, who came to have a great deal of autonomy. It was during the early period of the Abassid rule that the Islamic world became a centre for education, literature, philosophy, science and medicine. The House of Wisdom was created in Baghdad, serving as a library and educational centre. Great works from around the world were translated into Arabic and stored there and scholars, both Muslim and non-Muslim, came to translate, study and discuss.

Despite early prosperity, it was under the rule of the Abassids that the empire began to gradually fracture. Some of the outer reaches were taken over by various parties who had broken away from the caliphate. The local emirs became stronger and stronger until their territories became states in their own right and were ruled with complete autonomy by hereditary rulers. The power of the caliph's Mamluks, soldiers who had originally been imported as slaves to serve the caliph, had grown over the years until in the year 935 the role of Amir al-Umara, Commander of the Commanders, was created for the true holder of power, the head of the army. Thus by the middle of the tenth century, the caliphs had lost much of their authority and were to all intents and purposes nominal figureheads. The real authority was exercised by the emirs, many of them Mamluks, who treated the caliphs as puppets and controlled the succession.

The Koran

The Qur'an, or Koran, literally means "the recitation" and is considered by Muslims to be the word of God. It was revealed to Muhammad over a period of time from 610 until his death. Muhammad went on to preach the Koran to his followers, many of whom memorized it. After Muhammad's death, his successor, Abu Bakr, ordered that a written copy of the Koran be compiled. This text was then passed on to the next caliph, Umar, and on his death to his daughter, Muhammad's widow, Hafsa. The next caliph, Uthman, noticed that differences in dialect were causing disagreements, so he ordered that a standardized version of the text be created. A definitive version was produced and all other versions of the Koran were declared invalid and destroyed. It is this standard version of the Koran that has been used ever since.

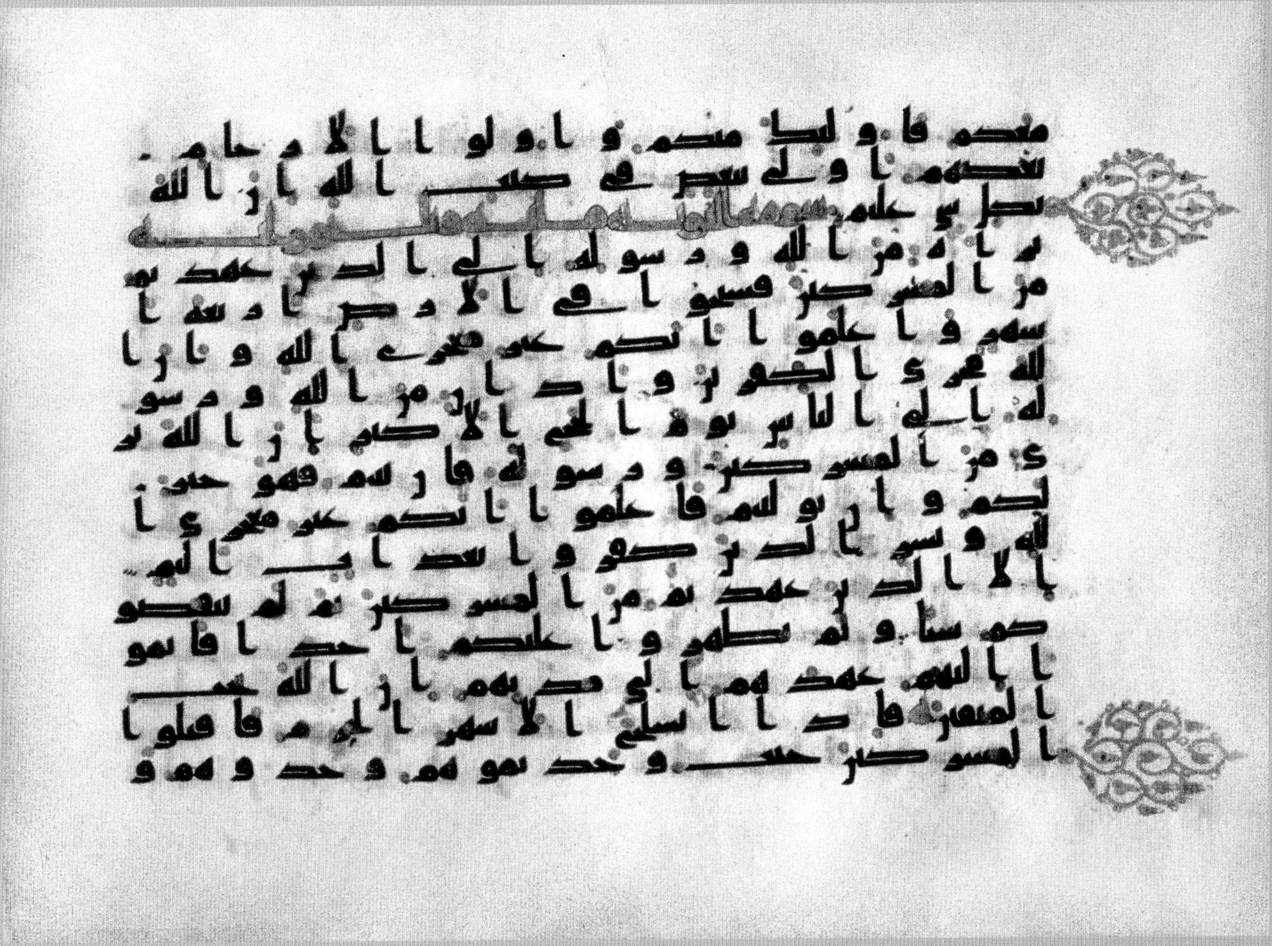

HIC FECERVN:PRANDIVM

CHAPTER

4

"WHEN THE WORDS
COME, THEY ARE
MERELY EMPTY SHELLS
WITHOUT THE MUSIC.
THEY LIVE AS THEY ARE
SUNG, FOR THE WORDS
ARE THE BODY AND
THE MUSIC THE SPIRIT."

**HILDEGARD OF BINGEN
(1098–1179)**

han þat Aprill loþe his schoures sote
þe drought of March haþe pad to þe rote.
And baþes euery veyne in suche lycoure.
Of whiche vtue engendir is þe floure.
Whan zephyrus eke wᵗ his swete breþe.
Inspired haþe in euy holte & heþie.
The tendre croppes & þe zonge sonne.
Haþe in þe ram his half cours ronne.
And smal foules maken melodye.
þat slepen al nyʒt wiþ open yhe.

So priklep hem nature in þer corages.
Than longen folke to gone one pilgrimages.
And palmeres for to seeke straungere stroudes.
To ferne halowes cowþe in sundre londes.
And specyally from euy shyires ende.
Of ingelond to Canterburi þei wende
The holy blissful martir for to seke.
That hem haþ holpen whan þei were seke.
It befel þan in þat sesone vpon a daie.
In Suthewerke att ye tabard as J laie.
Redi to wende on my pilgremage.
To Canterburie wiþ ful deuoute corage.
At nyʒte was come in to þat hostellerie
wel nyne and twente on a companye.
Of sundre folke be auenture yfalle
In felaushipe & Pilgrimes were þei alle.
Þᵗ toward Canterburi þai wolde ride
The chambres & stables weren wyde
And wele weren esede att þe beste.
An sþortly whan þe son was to ryste
So had J spoken wᵗ hem euythone
þat J was of her felawshep anone.
And maade forward erly for to ryse
To take oure waie þer as J zowe deuyse
Bot napeles while J haue tyme & space
Er þat J forþer in þis tale pace.

MEDIEVAL
CULTURE

OPPOSITE This page is from the Prologue of Geoffrey Chaucer's most famous work, *The Canterbury Tales*, a collection of stories told by a group of pilgrims to pass the time on their journey. Chaucer, who wrote the text at the end of the 14th century, used the stories and his characters to mock English society and the Church (see Translations, page 160).

Music in the Middle Ages

Until the twelfth century, the Gregorian chant was the most popular style of music in Middle Ages Europe. It was monophonic, meaning that it was a single melody unaccompanied by any instrument. This liturgical chant was sung in complete unison by the members of religious orders or by male church choirs.

Plainchants such as the Gregorian chant had been passed on orally until the early tenth century, when the first musical notations were written. These early notations used neumes, a number of specific symbols that indicated the notes and rhythm of the chant. However, they often did not show the precise note or rhythm to be sung but, instead, gave an idea of the overall form of the music. Neumes were used in various forms until the eleventh century, when the four-line staff – which evolved into the five-line staff we still use today.

Towards the end of the ninth century chants became more complex, with the addition of another voice singing above the main tune giving birth to the first harmonies. Later, towards the end of the tenth century, this basic harmony was further developed. The original melody would be sung slowly with the notes being held at length. Between each of the original notes another singer would sing a number of different notes, giving a much more complex sound. These polyphonic chants continued to develop throughout the Middle Ages and became a rich and vibrant sound.

Music was not just liturgical, but also secular. In the twelfth and thirteenth centuries troubadours travelled in France, Italy, Spain and Germany, usually singing their own songs of chivalry, war and courtly love. Many troubadours moved from place to place but some had a patron, usually a nobleman or noblewoman, with whom they would stay for a prolonged time. Troubadours came from many walks of life, ranging from dukes to tradesmen. The Duke of Aquitaine, Eleanor of Aquitaine's grandfather, whose work still survives today, was the first known troubadour.

The troubadour's song was often accompanied by an instrument, with the harp being a favoured one. Troubadours also played the lute, viol, fiddle and stringed instruments, such as the cittern, the mandolin or the psaltery. In the Middle Ages a large range of woodwind and percussion instruments was also available. These instruments included flutes, pipes, recorders, bagpipes, tambourines, drums and cymbals. Many of these instruments are the forerunners of our modern day instruments.

Medieval Literature

The literature of the Middle Ages encompassed many different subject matters. All manner of manuscripts were written, from tomes of fables to epic poetry

and military treatises to religious tracts. Early books would have been written by hand in careful script on parchment or vellum. Some, such as the ninth-century Book of Kells, would have been painstakingly illustrated with elaborate, decorative illumination.

Book covers would have been made of any number of materials from plain wood or leather to ornately carved ivory inset with gems. Books were a symbol of wealth and considered very precious possessions indeed.

In monasteries scriptoriums would have existed solely for the copying of text and the creation of books, both religious and secular. As Latin was the language the monks used, many of the early works were in Latin. There were many religious works, ranging from the Bible to papal writing such as the *Dialogues* of Pope Gregory I. There were also instructional works and prayer books.

ſalteaꝛ en un mōꞇe aó ꝓſꞇar ꞇ llı ꞇolleꝛon quanꞇo ꞇraꞇa

Some of the most popular religious works of the time were the many versions of the Book of Hours, which would include prayers and other religious material. Many would be lavishly illustrated with illuminations and religious scenes.

Many of the early works of the Middle Ages began life as stories passed down orally from generation to generation. Tales such as *Beowulf*, an Anglo-Saxon epic poem written in Old English which dates from around the eighth century, and the early Icelandic sagas, would probably have begun in this fashion. Rather than being written in Latin, they were written in the vernacular.

During the High Middle Ages the population became fascinated by ideals such as courtly love. Troubadours travelled from court to court, singing their songs of chivalry, courtly love and valour. Though these tales

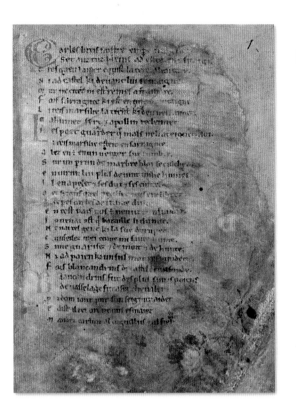

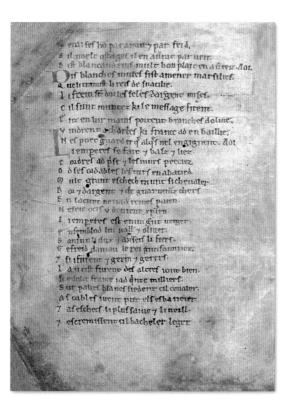

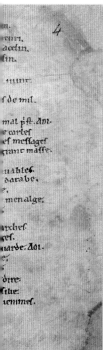

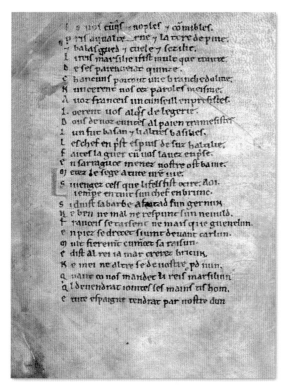

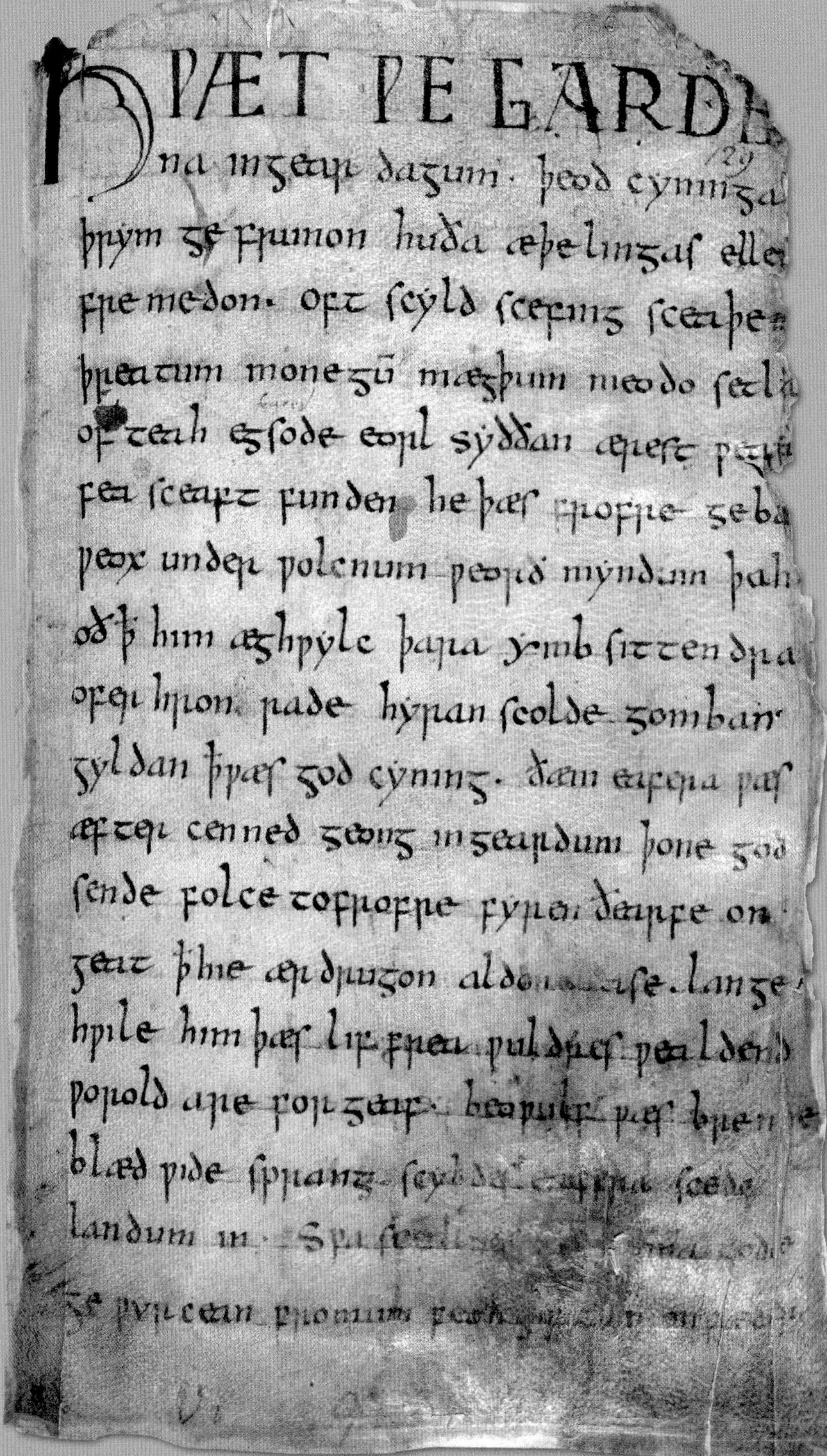

RIGHT Many stories, such as *Beowulf*, were handed down by word of mouth and not written down until much later. The first page of a 10th-century version of the poem is shown here.

were sung for an audience, they were also written down and kept in chansonniers, or songbooks. The works of William IX, Duke of Aquitaine (1071–1127), are the earliest troubadour songs that survive today.

Popular secular works during the period dealt with many themes, including war (*Song of Roland*, *Poem of the Cid*), legend and mythology (*The Mabinogian*, *Le Morte d'Arthur*), travel (*Travels of Marco Polo*, *The Canterbury Tales*) and courtly love (*De Amore*).

Not all medieval works were religious or fictitious. In the Islamic world many of the ancient Greek and Roman texts were translated into Arabic. Muslim philosophers, physicians and scholars then built on these texts and wrote their own treatise on subjects such as medicine, alchemy and algebra. Many were later translated in western Europe and were studied and researched and further discoveries and developments were also written about.

One of the most important inventions of the Middle Ages was the printing press. This one machine would eventually be responsible for bringing news and information to the masses and thus shaping the course

of history. Johannes Gutenberg is credited as being the inventor of the first printing press with movable letters. Using an alloy he had invented to make the letters and oil-based ink, he created the perfect formula for the early mass-production of books. He is best remembered for the Gutenberg Bible, the 42-line Bible printed on his printing press in 1456.

The Bayeux Tapestry

The Bayeux Tapestry is one of the most important and well-known works of art to have survived from the Medieval era. A work of enormous skill, it has priceless value as a piece of art in itself and is equally valuable as one of the great historical records of the Middle Ages

However, despite its name, it is not actually a tapestry but an embroidered cloth. Annotated in Latin and surrounded by a border featuring mythological figures and scenes from Aesop's Fables, the tapestry tells the story of the Norman conquest of England, culminating in the Battle of Hastings. It depicts Duke Harold Godwinson, brother-in-law of King Edward the Confessor, who was shipwrecked in Ponthieu in 1064. Following his rescue

by William, Duke of Normandy, Harold is shown swearing to support William in his quest to succeed Edward the Confessor as King of England – a promise that he was later to break. Harold is then shown returning to England and being acclaimed as king after Edward's death. The tapestry approaches this piece of history from the Norman perspective, attempting to justify the invasion launched by William to claim what he believed was rightfully his.

It is embroidered in wool yarn on an unbleached linen background. The stitching took two forms; the first was outline stitching which was used for the lettering and figure outlines; the second was a method now known as "Bayeux stitch" – threads were laid across the fabric and held in place using more laid thread at right angles to the original thread, which was stitched to the material at intervals. The second type of stitching was used to fill the figures. The linen panels were then stitched together, the seams being covered with more embroidery. Originally, it would have been longer than the 70 metres (231 feet) we can see today; there is a missing piece, possibly depicting William's coronation. However, there is no actual record of what it showed.

There are several intriguing events shown in the tapestry, one of which is a section showing an unknown clergyman caressing or, perhaps, hitting a woman's face. It has been speculated that the legend above, which states "*ubi unus clericus et Aelfgyva*" ("where a

cleric and Aelfgyva") refers to a scandal that was well known at the time. In addition to this woman, generally referred to as "The Mysterious Lady", only two other women are shown on the main narrative of the tapestry, which depicts a total of 623 people. One is believed to be Edith, wife of Edward the Confessor and sister of King Harold, and another woman is shown fleeing from a burning building at Hastings.

The tapestry is thought to have been commissioned around the 1070s by William the Conqueror's half-brother, Bishop Odo of Bayeux, in honour of William's great victory of the Battle of Hastings, although a romantic French legend has it that the tapestry was commissioned and created by Queen Matilda, William's wife, and her ladies-in-waiting. Some historians believe that it was finished in time for the dedication of Bayeux Cathedral in 1077 and most agree that it was completed no later than 1092. It is generally thought that it was created in England by English embroiderers because it is similar to other English works of the period and the Latin text on the tapestry contains hints of Anglo-Saxon.

In 1476 it was recorded that the tapestry was displayed in Bayeux Cathedral for a week, once a year (to celebrate the Feast of St John the Baptist), but there is no record of when this practice started. Today it can be seen at the Centre Guillaume le Conquérant in Normandy, France, and a number of replicas are on display in various parts of the world.

RIGHT Bishop Odo of Bayeux, seen here blessing the food and wine at a banquet, was William's half brother. Odo fought at the Battle of Hastings alongside his brother and was made Earl of Kent in 1067.

hIC FECERVN: PRANDI

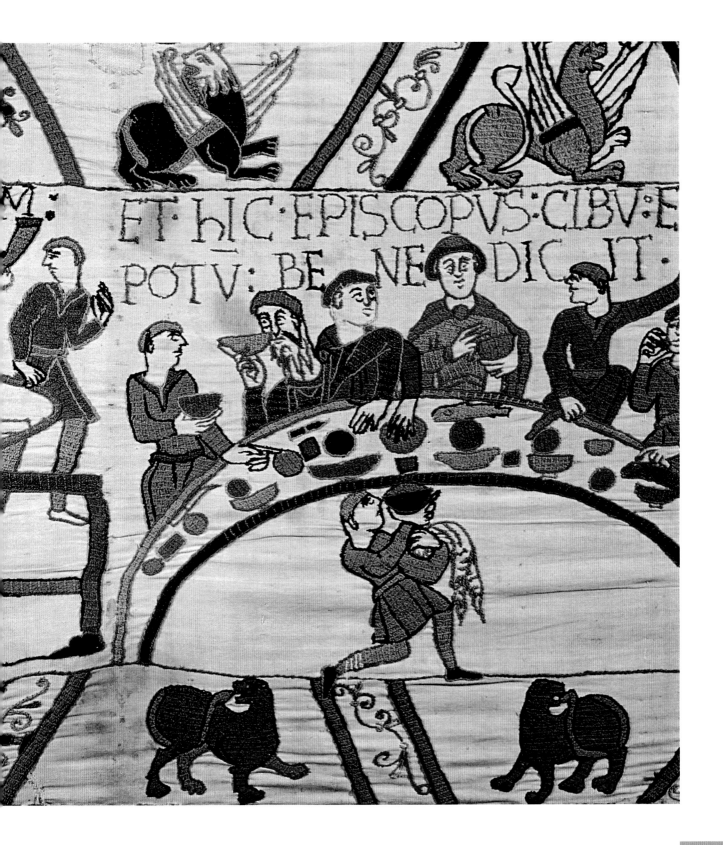

ET·HIC·EPISCOPVS·CIBV·E POTV: BE NE DIC IT·

Buona pulcella fut eulalia Bel auret corps bellezour anima
Voldrent lauintre li dō inimi Voldrent lafaire diauле seruir
Elle nont eskoltet les mals conselliers Quelle dō raneiet chi maent sus enciel
Ne por or ned argent neparamenz por manatce regiel nepreiement
Niule cose non lapouret omq pleier La polle sempre n amast lo dō menestier
E poro fut p̄sentede maximiien Chi rex eret a cels dis soure pagiens
Il li enortet dont lei nonq chielt Qued elle fuiet lo nom xp̄iien
Ellent adunet lo suon element Melz sostendreiet les empedementz
Quelle perdesse sa uirginitet Poros furet morte a grand honestet
Enz enl fou lo getterent com arde tost Elle colpes n auret poro nos coist
A czo nos uoldret concreidre li rex pagiens Ad une spede li roueret tolir le chief
La domnizelle celle kose n contredist Volt lo seule lazsier si ruouet krist
In figure de colomb uolat a ciel Tuit oram que por nos degnet preier
Qued auuisset de nos xp̄s mercit Post la mort & a lui nos laist uenir
Par souue clementia

RITHMUS TEUTONICUS DE PIE MEMORIE HLUDUICO REGE
FILIO HLUDUICI AEQ REGIS

Einan kuning uueiz ih Heizsit her hluduig
Ther gerno gode thionot Ih uueiz her imos lonot
Kind uuarth her faterlos Thes uuarth imo sarbuot
Holoda inan truhtin Magaczogo uuarth her sin
Gab her imo dugidi Fronisc githigini
Stual hier in urankon So bruche her es lango
Thaz gideilder thanne Sar mit karlemanne

xviii

Cantica uirginis eulalie concin...
gin p̄cui clangere carmine m...
melodia atq laude mirabor...
eximium uocib ministrabo suf...
ingeniu fuchsse fletu co pellas...
uente subtempore Nonder thor...
equi flamisignis inplicuit Mox...
hicerat eulalie Lacteol&s celse...
displicuit Ac idcirco stellescel...
ut prega quisibi laeti pangunt...
dordemus innocuos ut nob pia...
ac adquirat auxiliu Cui sol&...
quoq mud& acriminib Inferat...
lumnis aureoli do famulanti...
alibus homine p̄agens Ang&spirc...
ratu sceleru luxuria criminu Impiu...
xp̄s famulos unde princeps inferorū flammi...
ustorm& struens simul iuuu&c terminou...
Dot sanguine& sulphur uapmes clg...
n cor mentis aufer fidelibus coll...
uibinibus

As the tapestry was commissioned by the victors, it depicts events from the Norman perspective. Despite this bias, it is a valuable primary historical source, giving not only details of the Norman Conquest, but also information about weaponry, apparel and myths of the time. The tapestry was subjected to a well-intentioned restoration attempt in the last century, which resulted in modern stitching filling in the gaps in the fabric, with dubious accuracy. However, for all its faults, both material and in historical veracity, the Bayeux Tapestry remains one of the true treasures of history.

Travel

There were many reasons for travel in the Middle Ages. Whether a merchant travelling to sell his goods, a nobleman journeying to inspect his holdings, or a pilgrim hoping to secure his place in heaven, people from different walks of life would have cause to travel.

Medieval kings and rulers would have been prodigious travellers. They and their household, and sometimes even their courts, would travel around their lands to deal with internal issues and maintain control of their dominions. They would also journey to other lands, mostly for reasons of politics, family or war. The nobles would also often have widespread estates and would spend much of their time travelling between holdings, again to maintain control of their possessions and make their presence felt. When the king and his nobles travelled, every effort would be made to make sure that they were as comfortable as possible, both on the road and at night. At night, a king would be within his rights to stay at the dwelling of any of his vassals, which would entail no mean expense for the vassal.

Travellers would sometimes embark on journeys for religious reasons. Members of the holy orders, such as Saint Augustine, would travel to pagan lands to try and convert the inhabitants to Christianity. Pilgrims would travel to holy sites such as Jerusalem or Rome. Pilgrimages were often made on foot with people from all walks of life – whether the free peasant or the nobleman – making the journey. There was another religious reason for travel, and that was the Crusades. Crusaders would travel vast distances to the Holy Land by foot, horse or ship. These journeys could take years and the hardships encountered, such as starvation,

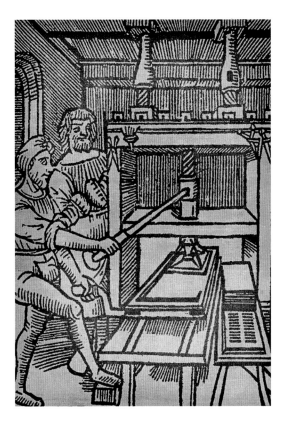

enemy attack and disease, often resulted in the crusader dying a horrible death in a strange land, far away from home and loved ones.

Travel for reasons of trade was common during the Middle Ages. Routes, such as the Silk Road into Asia, were well-trodden paths that allowed luxury good to be imported from the east. However, not all merchants went so far afield. Many went from town to town selling their wares, which would be transported in a cart or by horse. Along with trade came exploration with explorers going increasingly further afield. One such adventurer was Marco Polo, who documented his travels and experiences in Asia, giving us the classic text *The Travels of Marco Polo*.

While travelling, it was preferable to find shelter overnight. Sleeping out in the open could leave a traveller open to attack. Monasteries and convents often catered for travellers. Also, hostels and inns could sometimes be found, especially along the pilgrimage routes. People would also sometimes open up their homes to travellers to give them a place to sleep for the night, even though at times that would be a spot in the barn.

The mode of travel was dependent on wealth. The poor, who could not afford a mount, would walk, whereas the better off would travel by horseback. Mules, asses and donkeys could also be used to transport people and goods. The wealthiest could travel in a covered wagon. Water travel was undertaken in a variety of different vessels. On rivers, barges could be used to get from town to town. At sea, the Vikings used their distinctive longboats for raiding, trading and exploring. Western Europeans often used sail-driven ships to take their soldiers to war or to transport their goods. During the crusades, because of the large numbers of men and horses being transported by ship, it was necessary for the vessels to stop at land often to take on provisions and fresh water. This meant that travel by sea could be a long, drawn-out process. The advent of the magnetic compass in the late Middle Ages made travel by sea much easier because it was possible to navigate in poor visibility.

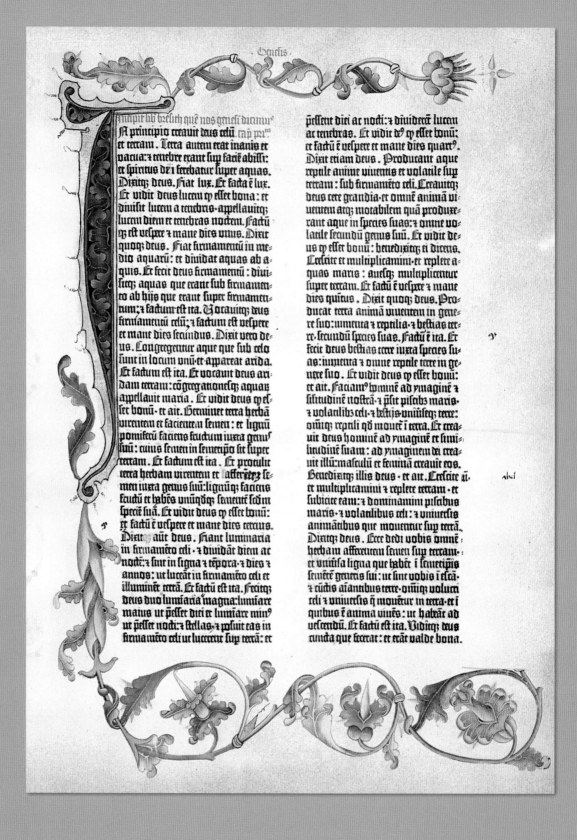

OPPOSITE AND RIGHT
The Gutenberg Bible was the first major book that was printed with movable type in the western world. Included here are the first two pages from the book of Genesis. Before the Gutenberg Bible was printed, there was no standard order for the text. Johann Gutenberg's version of the text was to become the foundation of subsequent versions.

Travel was not an easy undertaking. Most roads were in a terrible condition, making even the shortest journey arduous. The condition of the roads could lead to accidents such as a stumbling horse throwing its rider or a cart overturning, both of which often ended in injury or death. There were other dangers for travellers as well. Bandits and thieves would prey on the unwary traveller, and those travelling through enemy lands, such as pilgrims to the Holy Land, would be under constant threat of attack from enemy forces. At sea, the threat of piracy was always looming, as was the possibility of shipwreck. In fact, the dangers of travel were so rife that many never made it back home from their journeys, having lost their life along the way.

CHAPTER

5

"WAR IS DELIGHTFUL TO THOSE WHO HAVE NO EXPERIENCE OF IT."

DESIDERIUS ERASMUS
(c.1466–1536)

WAR AND CONQUEST

The Vikings

The Vikings originated from pagan Nordic tribes who lived in modern-day Scandinavia. Charlemagne's enlarged Frankish Empire bordered the land of the Danes, one of the pagan Nordic tribes who lived in modern-day Scandinavia. From these northern tribes came the Vikings.

Not all Scandinavians were Viking raiders; many were farmers and traders. However, it is the seafaring members of the tribes who have become most famous, due to their brutal attacks on coastal monasteries and towns and their trading and settlement expeditions. No-one knows what started the raids, though overpopulation in Scandinavia may have been a key factor. The hordes of booty and lack of defences at many of the sites attacked must also have been a significant draw.

A raid could involve just a few ships or a vast number sailing together presenting a formidable force that would strike terror into the hearts of the victims who, often taken by surprise, rarely had time to put together any kind of defence. The first recorded Viking raid in Britain was the sack of the abbey on Lindisfarne in 793. There was no warning of the attack and no chance for any defence to be made. The Vikings swept onto the island, killing and maiming as they went. They plundered the treasures held by the abbey and, once their killing spree was over, took the survivors as slaves. The attack was to be the start of centuries of

such raids and thus the Viking Age began. By the early 800s the Vikings had destroyed many of the coastal monasteries in the north of England and probably Scotland as well; no-one knows the exact number attacked because most were destroyed and with them any records. Ireland also suffered greatly at the hands of the Vikings; it was ravaged in the first half of the ninth century with many of its monasteries suffering the same fate of those in Scotland and England.

The Vikings were not only raiders, they were also traders, and they settled in various parts of Europe. In England, by the middle of the ninth century they had established settlements in York and Northumbria and, from there, they raided the rest of England. However, they were driven back in 877 and 878 by Alfred the Great of Wessex. Much of England was still in Viking hands, but Alfred's successors continued to fight them, though not always successfully. It would be almost 200 years before the Vikings were eventually defeated and driven away from England for the last time, in 1066 at Stamford Bridge.

In Ireland the Vikings founded a number of bases on sites of future cites, including Dublin and Limerick. They raided the rest of Ireland and further afield from these bases. In Scotland they settled on a number of the islands, including Shetland and Orkney, and on some of the mainland. Around 900 they settled in

ABOVE Viking raids on English coastal settlements were swift and often without warning.

Iceland and, from there, Greenland. They even went as far afield as North America, although never permanently settling there.

The Vikings did not content themselves with raiding just these northern lands. Raids are recorded in all corners of the civilized world. They raided Francia (the kingdom of the Franks) on numerous occasions during the ninth and tenth centuries, although their only settlement was established in the tenth century in a region that was to become Normandy. They raided the Iberian Peninsula on a few occasions as well. In the east, they went into Russia and settled in various locations, including Kiev. They also settled along the Baltic Sea.

There have been many suggestions as to why the Viking age ended. The most likely reason is that by the end of the eleventh century many countries had a central government and this coupled with widespread conversion to Christianity made Europe more stable. Added to that, potential targets were becoming increasingly better fortified and defended. With the advent of the Little Ice Age affecting the cold northern waters, raiding was no longer such an inviting pursuit. The one thing that made all of the Viking conquests possible was the Viking longship. These revolutionary ships were designed to be long and narrow with a shallow hull so that they could float in shallow water and land straight onto a beach. This design meant that they were not confined to the sea and could be used on rivers as well, attacking targets that might have thought themselves safe because of their location by water that was not deep enough for most ships to traverse. As the longships were symmetrical, they were easy to sail in either direction without turning. The ship would have been decked with oars along almost the whole length. The oars and sail would be used to power the ship. Longships came in many different lengths, with some holding up to 120 warriors.

Life on board would have been hard, especially in the harsh weather of the North Sea. While they were at sea the Vikings would have slept on deck, probably in sleeping bags made of sealskin, which would keep them

dry on the wet deck. The sail could have been taken down and used as a tentlike cover for extra protection from the elements. If they were near shore, they may have slept on land instead. They would have eaten sun-dried fish, which would keep for a long time without spoiling. They would also have eaten bread and water and supplies they had stolen while raiding.

The Vikings navigated using the stars or the sun and also by using directions from others who had sailed the route before.

However, the Vikings should not be remembered just for their brutal assaults. They were great traders with huge trade networks and were skilled craftsmen who not only built ships but also created beautiful jewellery and other items out of metal, bone and wood.

The Norman Conquest

By the middle of the eleventh century, the Duchy of Normandy in France had expanded because of a series of wars during which it occupied neighbouring territories.

It had also become so powerful that it functioned almost completely autonomously. England, on the other hand, by the start of the eleventh century had been devastated by war. Throughout Aethelred II's reign the Vikings had fought to take the country. Aethelred's death in 1016 was followed swiftly by that of his son, Edmund II, after which the Danish King Canute became king of all of England. His rule eventually led to prosperity and peace. However, Canute died in 1035 and his sons were not good rulers. Therefore, in 1042 Edward the Confessor, one of Aethelred II's sons, assumed the throne.

It is with Edward the Confessor that the story of the Norman Conquest begins. Edward was the son of Aethelred II and his wife, who was the sister of Richard II, Duke of Normandy. During his reign Edward appointed Normans to many powerful positions in England and possibly even promised the throne to Duke William of Normandy. However, William was not the only person in line for the English throne. Edward died without legitimate offspring in 1066 and it is said that, while on

ABOVE LEFT
The iconic Viking longship was a great feat of craftsmanship.

ABOVE The Vikings arrived at Lake Ladoga in Russia, possibly as early as the 8th century. Scandinavian settlers would not only have been warriors but also traders, farmers and craftsmen and settlements such as this were hives of activity.

RIGHT The Battle of Hastings was a hard-fought battle. It started soon after dawn and was not concluded until after dark with the defeat of Harold's remaining housecarls, who made a fruitless last stand.

his deathbed, he named as his heir Harold Goodwinson, the Earl of Essex. Harold was duly crowned king. However, according to the Norman version of events, Harold had been sent to Normandy in 1064 to confirm Edward's promise of the throne to William. While there, Harold apparently swore an oath to uphold William's right to the throne of England. If this was indeed true it means that Harold was violating his oath when he allowed himself to be crowned king.

Harold's short reign was fraught with violence. William was not his only rival for the crown. Harald Hardrada of Norway also staked his claim and, joining forces with Tostig, Harold's exiled brother, he invaded the north of England. Harold swiftly marched north from London to meet them and on 25 September 1066 battle commenced at Stamford Bridge in Yorkshire. Harold had managed the almost 320-kilometre (200-mile) journey in just four days, which meant that he gained the element of surprise. In one of the bloodiest battles on English soil the Viking force was virtually annihilated. The survivors left, after pledging never to invade again.

Harold's troubles were not over, though: just three days after the battle of Stamford Bridge, William of Normandy landed with his forces on the south coast of England. Harold had to take his exhausted, battle-weary troops quickly back south again to face William. On 14 October the two forces met near Hastings. What followed would be one of the defining moments of British history. The battle lasted most of the day and was not easily won. Eventually, late in the afternoon, Harold was killed, supposedly by an arrow or other weapon through the eye, and by dusk the remainder of his army had fled. William stood victorious.

His next move was to march on London and, after some resistance, the English surrendered. He was crowned King of England on Christmas Day 1066 in Westminster Abbey. For the next few years there was sporadic resistance to Norman rule across the country. These rebellions were put down and Norman supremacy was firmly established.

It is one thing to take a country, but another thing entirely to keep it. William managed not only to keep his new territory but to firmly control it as well, even though much of the time he was absent. One of his first moves was to dispossess almost all the native landholders

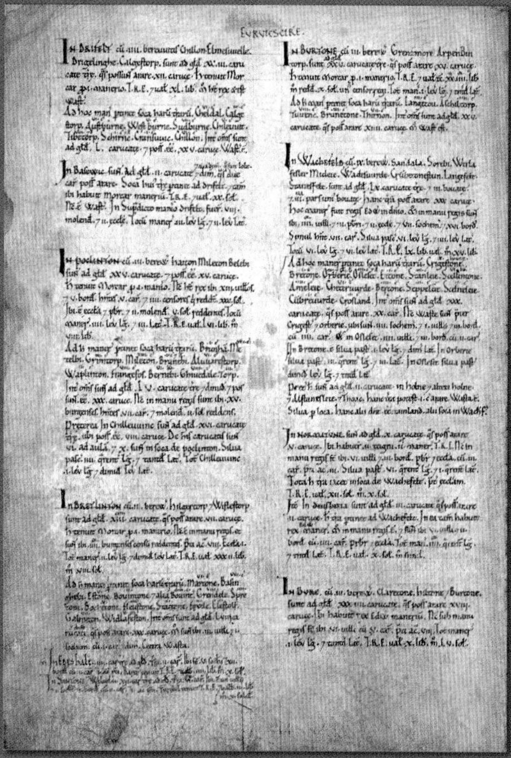

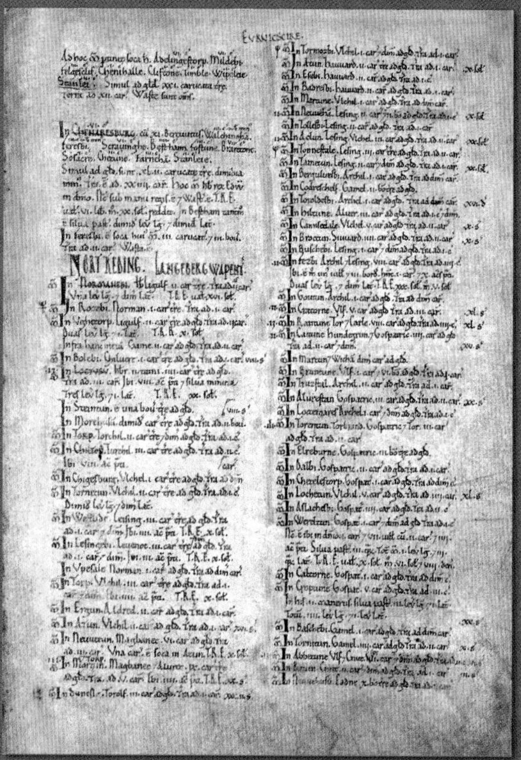

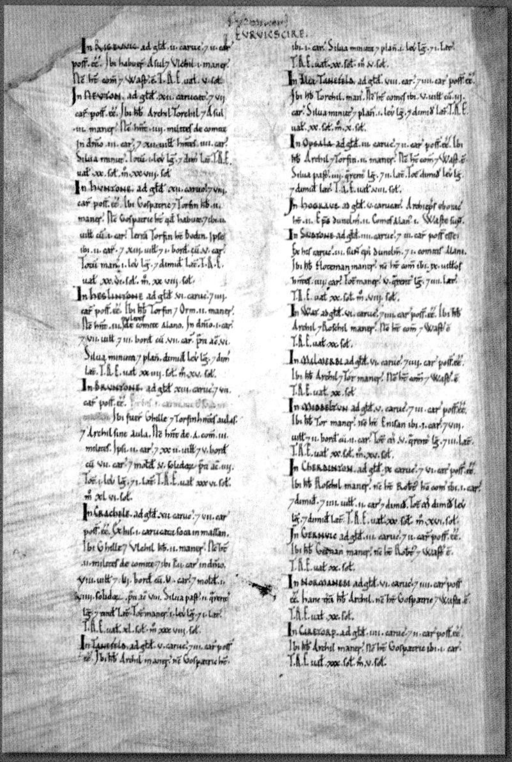

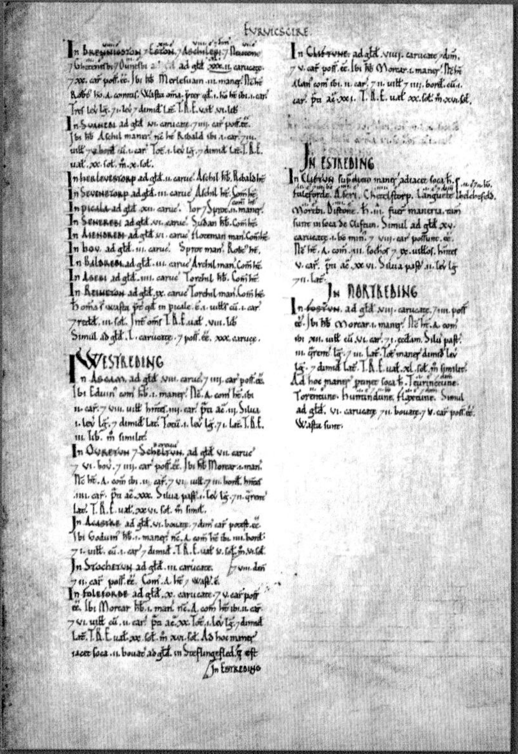

NORT TREDING. LANGEBERG WAPENT.

WESTTREDING

IN ESTREDING

IN NORTREDING

OPPOSITE The *Domesday Book* was the record of the survey of England and Wales done on the orders of William the Conqueror. It was completed in 1086. The pages included here cover the taxable resources of Yorkshire.

RIGHT Queen Matilda holds a charter.

and bequeath their land to his followers. William also introduced feudalism and so claimed all the land in the country as his, giving it out in return for services to the crown, such as military service. Almost all high-ranking positions in the country, including those in the Church, were given to fellow Normans. Castles sprang up all over the island to help subjugate the native people. The most famous of these is the White Tower of the Tower of London, built in 1078.

Perhaps one of William's greatest achievements was the Domesday survey, which is now known as the *Domesday Book*. This census and survey was completed in 1086 and its aim was mainly to discover tax liabilities. William was determined not to miss out on a single penny, so this fully comprehensive survey even included details of every head of livestock owned.

The Norman conquest was to change all aspects of English life, from the customs and culture to the politics. The language also changed – English was no longer used in official documents, replaced by Anglo-Norman French, which was also the language of the ruling classes, leaving English to be spoken by the peasantry. The course of the nation was also affected, with England eventually becoming a key player in the wars and politics of Europe.

Norman England

By the end of William I's reign, England had been completely Normanized with most important official posts being held by Normans. The English upper classes had been dispossessed and the last remaining English earl had been executed for treason in 1076.

Under the feudal system, William granted lands to a number of tenants-in-chief. Around the country castles had risen up as administrative centres and as fortresses from which to subjugate the people and rebellions had been put down. The Church was under the control of Norman bishops, so William controlled not only the secular but also the religious elements of the realm.

Thus England in 1087, the year of William's death, little resembled the England he had conquered two decades earlier. This new Norman England was inherited by his son William Rufus, who became William II of England. As the second living son, William Rufus inherited England, the conquered territory, and his older brother, Robert Curthose, inherited the Duchy of Normandy. William's

reign was not without incident. There were nobles with holdings in both states, and preferring not to serve two masters, they decided that Normandy and England should be ruled by one ruler, Robert. Therefore, in 1088 they instigated a rebellion against William. The rebellion failed, in part because Robert chose to stay in Normandy. Despite this setback, Robert still wished to rule both England and Normandy, as did William. However, in a strange twist of fate, William got his way. In 1096 Robert joined the First Crusade. To pay for his mission he borrowed 10,000 marks from William, leaving him Normandy as security. William ruled both states until 1100, when he was killed in the New Forest while out hunting.

William's younger brother, Henry, who had been with William in the New Forest at the time of this death, quickly secured the treasury and took the throne of England

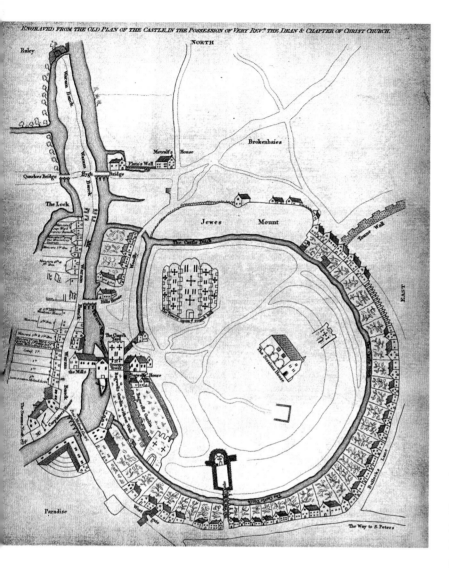

ABOVE Possibly Oxford Castle, this plan shows how a natural feature such as a river could be exploited for the defence of medieval buildings.

to become Henry I. Robert returned from crusade just weeks after William's death and unsuccessfully invaded England in July 1101. This led to Henry going on the offensive and he finally defeated Robert in 1106. Henry was at last able to join Normandy and England under his sole rule.

Henry was an able and diplomatic ruler. During most of his reign there was peace in England. He married a Scottish princess of Anglo-Saxon descent, thus joining the Norman and Anglo-Saxon royal lines. He had two legitimate children, Matilda, who married Holy Roman Emperor Henry V, making her Empress Matilda, and

William Adelin. In 1120 William died when his ship went down in the English Channel. This left Henry with no legitimate male heir. He took the unusual step of forcing his barons to swear allegiance to his daughter Matilda and making her his heir. To strengthen her position, Henry then brought about the marriage of the 25-year-old Matilda, now a widow, to Geoffrey Plantagenet, the 14-year-old son of Fulk of Anjou, an old enemy.

Despite his efforts, when Henry died in 1135 the succession was not straightforward. Although they had given their oath, many of the Norman barons did not back Matilda as queen. This is most likely because not only was she a woman but, at the time of Henry's death, she and Geoffrey had fallen out with Henry and were fighting against him. Also, when Henry died unexpectedly, Matilda was in Anjou and, although she left to take possession of Normandy, she was not able to reach England quickly upon news of his death. On the other hand Stephen of Blois, Henry's nephew, was in Boulogne and was able to sail speedily to England to claim the throne for himself. He was proclaimed king and crowned on 22 December 1135. His actions were to lead to almost two decades of bloodshed as civil war tore England apart.

Stephen was a brave and gallant knight, but a weak king. In the early years of his reign he gave up land in the north to King David of Scotland and paid off Empress Matilda's husband, Geoffrey of Anjou, in an attempt to keep Normandy. In Wales he was seemingly ineffectual in quelling rebellion. In 1139 Empress Matilda invaded England to reclaim the kingdom she believed to be rightfully hers. In the bloody years that followed, England was in disarray. Many of the barons, concerned more with their own interests than those of the country, changed sides at will. Castles that had not been sanctioned by the monarch were built and anarchy reigned.

In 1141 Stephen was captured and deposed in favour of Matilda. However, Matilda was extremely unpopular with the people and she was never crowned. When Stephen was exchanged for her half-brother, Robert of Gloucester, he took the throne again. The war dragged on for the next few years, with no-one really gaining the upper hand in England. In Normandy it was a different story: Geoffrey eventually took the whole province to become Duke of Normandy in 1144.

Although Matilda returned to Normandy in 1148 and never again went back to England, her son Henry continued the fight. He invaded England in 1153. That same year Stephen's son and heir died and Stephen agreed to a peace treaty. He would keep the throne for his lifetime and would be succeeded by Henry. Thus, when Stephen died in October 1154 Henry claimed the throne unopposed to become King Henry II of England.

Medieval Fortifications

One iconic sight from the Middle Ages that still towers over many landscapes today is the castle. It was not a new invention, but during the Middle Ages castle construction became widespread. When the Normans conquered England in 1066 they set about a programme of castle-building to aid in the subjugation of the defeated Anglo-Saxons.

Their castles followed the motte-and-bailey design, which consisted of a large mound (motte), upon which the keep and its defences would be constructed, encircled by a ditch. An enclosed bailey, a kind of courtyard, would be constructed at the bottom of the mound. The keep could either be built of wood or stone. Where viable, the ditch could be filled with water, often from a nearby river, to become a moat. A drawbridge would be installed to allow the moat to be crossed.

The castle keep was a fortified tower that served as the last line of defence should a castle fall. It would usually be the most fortified part of the castle and the walls could be many metres thick. Norman keeps, such as the White Tower at the Tower of London, tended to be square and could contain accommodation, storage rooms, latrines, a chapel and a great hall. The keep would also usually contain everything necessary to withstand a siege, including a well for fresh water. As the Middle Ages progressed some keeps became increasingly ornate with elaborate towers and stonework.

Over time, the use of stone as a building material became more prevalent and the motte-and-bailey castle was, in some areas, superseded by other designs. In Europe stone castles were built on low-lying land to take advantage of natural defences. A number were surrounded by water – often on an island in a river or lake or by the side of a river, using diverted river water as a moat – with the only means of entry being the drawbridge. Others were built in boggy terrain, making attacking them extremely difficult.

Stone-built castles were also often constructed on natural high ground, such as cliffs or hill summits,

removing the necessity of building a motte. Crusader castles tended to be built in such a way. One of the most famous examples was Crac des Chevaliers in Tripoli, which was used by the Knights Hospitaller from the twelfth century. Built on a hill over 600 metres (2,000 feet) high, the primary function of the castle was to be a defendable stronghold. To this end, it was defended by an inner and outer wall, both with towers interspaced along their length. The four formidable towers of the inner ward, surrounded by a steep glacis, or artificial slope, would have housed the Knights Hospitaller. Inside the inner walls was a courtyard which contained a number of buildings, such as the chapel.

Crusader castles were not the only examples of magnificent stone-built castles. Edward I's ring of castles in Wales were also great feats of engineering and design. The most impressive example of these is perhaps Caernarfon Castle. Built at the mouth of the River Seiont from stone quarried locally, its polygonal towers

and battlements dominate the waterline. It was never intended to be purely for military use, but also to be used as a royal palace and centre of power and its architecture reflects this. As well as extensive defences, the castle also contained luxurious accommodation and ornate stonework. Although never finished, it is a testament to the skill of the architects and craftsmen of the period.

The medieval castle was often not just a stronghold, but also a home and administrative centre. Early castle life revolved around the hall, a large, high-ceilinged room where meals would be eaten and which would often serve as sleeping quarters as well. However, in later times, there would be more privacy, with the lord and lady of the castle having their own quarters, called the solar. The castle would not just house the lord and lady and their family, but a multitude of others as well. There would be servants and military personnel as well as any guests and their retinues. The castle was, therefore, a hive of activity from dawn until dusk. Religion played an

ABOVE LEFT Pope Urban II, who initiated the First Crusade.

ABOVE RIGHT The Knights Templar could be instantly recognized by the distinctive red cross on a white background displayed on their surcoat and shield. The addition of the cross dates from around the time of the second crusade.

important part of castle life, with many castles housing chapels where mass would be heard daily. There was also a more sinister side to castle life. Some castles contained underground dungeons and, as in Warwick Castle, an oubliette, a prison pit where the only access would be a hatch in a high ceiling.

With the advent of gunpowder and more and more powerful weapons, the castle as a defensive structure eventually became obsolete. However, ruins of these magnificent constructions can still be seen in many parts of the world. From the crusader castles in the Levant to Edward I's strongholds in Wales, their looming presence reminds us of a cruel and violent age long gone.

The First Crusade

During the eleventh century Muslim Turkish tribesmen, called the Seljuqs, were threatening the eastern borders of the Byzantine Empire. Throughout the middle of the century these warriors raided Anatolia. In 1071 the raids culminated in the Battle of Manzikert, which resulted in the destruction of the Byzantine army and the capture of the emperor, Romanus Diogenes.

Almost all of Anatolia was now open to the Turks, who laid waste to the land. On the fall of Antioch to the Turks in 1084, the empire lost its final foothold in Syria. The Turks were now a threat to the seat of Byzantine power itself, Constantinople. In 1095, with the loss of half his empire and the enemy practically at his gates, Emperor Alexius, despite being an eastern Christian, sought aid from the Latin Pope Urban II who agreed to aid him.

It was not only the worry of the Turkish threat that led to Urban taking action. Christian pilgrimages to Jerusalem had continued despite the city being in Muslim hands. However, with the incursion of the Seljuqs these pilgrimages, already risky affairs, were made perilous and sometimes nigh on impossible. It is entirely plausible that Urban's decision was influenced by this, along with the thought that should the Turks take the Eastern Empire, the West would be next.

One of the effects of the Gregorian reforms (see pages 69–78) was that by the end of the eleventh century the papacy had gained more influence over secular society. Therefore, towards the end of 1095, when Urban addressed the people at the Council of Clermont – an assembly convened by him in part to dicuss Alexius' calls

for aid – and called on them to help their fellow Christians in the east, the response was unprecedented. A religious fervour swept the continent and thousands of crusaders from across Europe descended on Constantinople. The cross they wore or sewed onto their vestments was a symbol of their calling.

A number of crusaders, under the leadership of a preacher called Peter the Hermit, arrived in Constantinople ahead of the main crusader armies. This "People's Crusade" was made up mainly of peasants and a number of knights who were not part of the main crusader armies. Although it was suggested that they

ABOVE A contemporary portrait of Saladin, dating from *c.* 1180.

remain in Constantinople to await the main armies, this motley bunch departed for the Holy Land in August 1096. Their crusade was not to be a success and the army was destroyed by the Turks at Civetot in Anatolia in October. Most of the few survivors went on to join the main crusader force.

In the meantime, the other crusader armies had been forming and travelling to Constantinople. There were four main armies in total. They left Constantinople in spring 1097 and arrived at Nicaea, the Seljuq capital, in May. After a short siege the city surrendered on 19 June. From Nicaea the crusaders marched on Antioch. In the months it took to reach the now Turkish stronghold, the crusader army suffered terribly. As the Seljuqs had followed a scorched-earth policy on their retreat from Nicaea, food and water were scarce and many died.

Life was no easier once they reached Antioch in October. During the prolonged siege that followed their arrival, food and water were still in short supply and disease was rife. The siege was finally broken on 3 June 1098, when treachery from within the city itself allowed the crusaders in. They took the main city very quickly, but the citadel held out. Unfortunately for the crusaders, once inside Antioch, they were themselves besieged by a Turkish relief force. However, these forces were beaten at the end of June and the citadel surrendered shortly afterwards. Following their victory the crusaders were again attacked, but by disease this time. Many died in the ensuing epidemic and that, along with squabbling among the leaders of the armies, led to the crusade being delayed.

At the start of 1099 the crusaders again set off, this time to their ultimate goal – the holy city of Jerusalem.

The first part of the crusade had been against the Seljuq Turks who had invaded the Byzantine Empire, but this part of the crusade would pit the crusaders against the Egyptian Fatimids, who had taken Jerusalem from the Seljuqs the year before.

The much reduced crusader force arrived at the gates of Jerusalem on 7 June. The city was finally taken by assault on 15 June and carnage followed, with the crusaders responsible for widespread slaughter.

Once Jerusalem was captured, a new kingdom of Jerusalem was established. This kingdom was one of the crusader states that were established in the wake of the First Crusade. These Christian territories also included the states of Antioch, Edessa and Tripoli. As for the surviving crusaders themselves, on their return home, they were feted as heroes. That said, their long absences had meant that, in some cases, they returned to political strife and further conflict. However, unlike many of their brethren, they did at least live to return home.

The Knights Templar

After the success of the First Crusade and the establishment of the crusader states, Jerusalem became a popular destination for Christian pilgrims. However, the crusader forces did not have a strong hold on their new territories, so the pilgrims were under constant threat of attack and many were killed.

In about 1119 Hugues de Payens, a French knight, brought together eight other knights and started a military religious order charged with the protection of the pilgrims. King Baldwin II of Jerusalem gave them accommodation in the Al-Aqsa Mosque, which was part of his Temple Mount palace, where the Temple of Solomon was said to have once stood. It is from this temple that the full name of the order comes – The Poor Knights of Christ and of the Temple of King Solomon.

The Templars were organized in the same way as a monastic order. They swore an oath of poverty, obedience and chastity and followed the prayer routine used by monks. However, they were not shut away from the world and were not obliged to devote time to study. They were fighters and that was their main responsibility.

Over the years, as the order grew so did the organizational structure. In each territory where the knights had a presence there was a master in charge of

all the knights in his territory. In overall command was the Grand Master, the first of whom was de Paynes. There were eventually three classes of Templar. First were the knights themselves. They had to be of aristocratic birth and were the only Templars allowed to wear the distinctive white surcoat with a red cross. When fighting they served as cavalry. Under the knights were the sergeants, who were of lower class and who fought or served as administrators or undertook a trade. Finally, there were the chaplains, who were the ordained priests of the order.

After 1119 little is known of the Templars until 1127, when de Paynes toured Europe to raise funds for the order. Then, at the 1128 Council of Troyes – a council called to settle disputes and discuss matters concerning the Church in France – the Church officially sanctioned the order, probably because of the patronage of Bernard de Clairvaux, one of the most influential clergymen of the era and the nephew of one of the original knights.

RIGHT Although most of the Christian army was exterminated at Hattin, King Guy of Jerusalem was captured and spared. He was eventually released in 1088, after a year of imprisonment in Damascus.

It was Clairvaux who with Hugues de Paynes in 1128 wrote what is now referred to as the Latin Rule. This code for the Templars stipulated the behaviour to which all members of the order should conform. It ruled on all aspects of daily life, including acceptable dress and how meals should be eaten.

In 1139 Pope Innocent II issued a papal bull dictating that the order would be solely under papal jurisdiction. This meant that the Templars were exempt from taxes and could pass through all borders without harassment. Although the Templars were individually poor, with the church's favour came great wealth. They became a charitable concern; money and land were donated to the order and many were keen to join. Thus their size and power increased so that by the middle of the twelfth century they owned land throughout Europe and the Holy Land.

As a fighting force the Templars were formidable and went from solely protecting pilgrims to participating in crusader battles, where they were frequently at the fore.

They would often lead the charge at the start of battle with the aim of breaking through enemy lines. As they seemingly embraced the idea of martyrdom in battle, they were an unremitting foe and there are many stories of small numbers of Templars fighting much larger enemy forces.

Although the Templars were prominent warriors, the majority of the order were non-combatants and worked in support roles. The Templars had military strength and a trusted reputation as well as a large infrastructure that straddled Europe and the Holy Land. This meant that they were seen as the perfect institution to entrust with valuables. Therefore, when crusaders ventured into the Holy Land they could put all their assets under Templar control to safeguard them for their eventual return. In the same vein, the pilgrims could deposit valuables into Templar care in their own country before setting out. The pilgrim would then be given a document detailing said valuables. On their journey, the pilgrims could visit Templars along the way, present the document and take

away funds, which would be taken off the value of the initial deposit. Thus the role of the Templars as early bankers was established.

Great power and wealth often bring great enemies and the Templars were no exception to the rule. There were rivalries with the other military orders of the time, such as the Hospitallers, and they also held the debts of many nobles, including King Philip IV of France. Considering the huge amount of money Philip owed the Templars, it seems obvious in hindsight why he decided to orchestrate their demise. However, there were also other considerations such as the Templar desire to create its own state, possibly in France, which along with their wealth and power, would make them a great threat. Therefore, on Friday 13 October 1307, a day the superstitious still fear, Jacques de Molay, the Templar Grand Master, and 60 of his knights were arrested in Paris. They were charged with a vast array of offences, including heresy, corruption, fraud and idolatry. Many were tortured into giving confessions. The French Pope

Clement V backed Philip and ordered that Templars in other countries be arrested and their wealth seized. In 1312, under pressure from the Pope, the Council of Vienne, which was a council convened by Clement V with the aim of dealing with the Templars and other Church mattters, officially dissolved the Knights Templar and much of their wealth was given to the Hospitallers. Many of the remaining Templars joined that order as well. On 18 March 1314 Jacques de Molay, the last Grand Master of the Templars, was burned at the stake. As he was licked by the flames, he declared that those who had condemned him would also die – and by the end of that year both Clement and Philip would be dead.

The Holy Land Crusades

Owing to their location and the way they were formed, the crusader states were often troubled. In 1144 the Turks took the northern state of Edessa, leaving neighbouring Antioch in a precarious position. When news of the loss reached Europe, Pope Eugenius III called for another crusade.

He was supported in this by one of the most influential churchmen of the time, Bernard de Clairvaux. This eloquent churchman recruited for the crusade in France and Germany, even managing to convince the reluctant Emperor Conrad III of Germany to join the cause. Thus, in 1147 two armies left separately for the Holy Land. The first, led by Conrad, left in May and the second, led by King Louis VII of France, left in June. Louis was accompanied by his wife, Eleanor of Aquitaine.

The Second Crusade had none of the glory of the First and more of the pain. The German army reached Constantinople in September and was persuaded to leave quickly by the Byzantine Emperor Manuel I Comnenus. He was worried about the trouble they might cause in his city, so was not enthusiastic about the prospect of the army staying in Constantinople for the weeks it would take for the French to arrive. Conrad, against Manuel's advice, decided to follow in the footsteps of the original crusaders and cross the Anatolian plateau rather than follow the coast.

The Germans arrived in Nicaea, where Conrad decided to split the army into two, sending one part along the coastal route suggested by Manuel. He then left with the rest of the army, following the original route. This was not a good decision and on 25 October, Conrad's army was almost completely annihilated by the Turks at Dorylaeum. Conrad and the few survivors returned to Nicaea. The other part of the German army fared little better and was also destroyed by the Turks.

Louis VII arrived in Constantinople in October and decided to take the coastal route. Conditions on the journey were harsh, especially crossing the mountains in winter. There was not enough food and the many Turkish attacks meant that the army lost much of its strength before it even reached the crusader states. The army arrived in Antioch in March 1148. There, instead of carrying on to fight for Edessa, the whole reason for the crusade, Louis decided to go straight on to Jerusalem.

In Jerusalem Louis was joined by Conrad and the remains of his army, and by Baldwin III, the King of Jerusalem. After some argument, they decided that Damascus, a sometime ally of Jerusalem, should be their target. However, the attack was badly planned and executed. After a four-day siege, with a Turkish force closing in, the crusaders decided to retreat and so the Second Crusade came to its inglorious conclusion.

In 1149, in the wake of the humiliating failure of the Second Crusade, the Turkish forces of Nur ad-Din attacked and took much of the lands of Antioch. Then in 1154 they took Damascus. This was a huge blow to Jerusalem because it meant that it was almost completely encircled by unified Muslim forces.

All eyes now turned towards Egypt and the weakened Fatmid Caliphate. Although the crusaders had taken the Fatmid city of Ascalon in 1153, that was to be their last great victory. Nur ad-Din had long wished to unify the Muslims and fight the crusaders as one, rather than repeat the uncoordinated retaliation that had led to the Muslim failure to stop the First Crusade. To reach this goal he had for a long time had his sights set on Egypt.

ABOVE Genghis
Khan in battle, from
a book by Rashid-
al-Din.

In 1164 and 1167 he sent one of his generals, Shirkuh, to Egypt. Both times Shirkuh was accompanied by his nephew, Saladin. Although on both these occasions Shirkuh's forces eventually withdrew, in 1168 he again returned and took power as vizier in 1169. On his death, that same year, Saladin assumed control of Egypt.

In 1174 Nur ad-Din died and Saladin claimed the right to be regent to Nur ad-Din's young heir. However, soon he gave up the claim and spent the next decade fighting to take control of Nur ad-Din's territories, which were held by a number of the Nur ad-Din's relatives. By 1186 Saladin had managed to unite Syria and Egypt under his leadership. This meant that, for the first time, the crusaders would be fighting a cohesive force united under one strong leader.

Saladin's success meant that Jerusalem and the remaining crusader territories were more isolated than ever. Jerusalem was also riven with internal conflict. Because of succession issues political intrigue was rife in the decades following the death of the great king, Baldwin III, in 1163. A childless, leper king was followed by an infant king who was, in turn, followed by a queen. There were no direct male heirs, so every succession

led to trouble within the kingdom. Then, in 1187, a truce with Saladin was broken and in July of that year he marched on Tiberias in the kingdom of Jerusalem. A large crusader army was raised and the two forces met on 4 July at the Horns of Hattin. The ensuing battle resulted in a crushing defeat for the Christians.

This defeat left the kingdom completely vulnerable so, by late September, Saladin had taken most of the coast, apart from Tyre, and many of the kingdom's great crusader strongholds, including Acre. Jerusalem surrendered in October and by 1189 the crusader states had been reduced to a few key strongholds, which included the cities of Antioch and Tripoli.

When the news of the fall of Jerusalem reached Europe, Pope Gregory VIII issued a papal bull calling for aid for Christians in the east. Crusaders from throughout Europe, from all walks of life, answered the call to arms. Richard I of England, Philip II of France – who were at war at the time – and Frederic I Barbarossa of Germany all took the cross. Richard and Philip set out for the Holy Land in July 1190, while Frederick had left a couple of months earlier. Richard conquered the island of Cyprus, establishing another crusader state – the Kingdom of Cyprus.

Frederick I, never made it to the Holy Land, as he died on the journey. His army had encountered problems with the Byzantines and Turks along the way, so it was a much depleted army – led by Frederick's son, Frederick, Duke of Swabia – that arrived at Acre in October 1190. By the time Richard and Philip arrived in the Holy Land in 1191, the Christians in the east had already begun to fight back against Saladin and had besieged the port of Acre. However, the Christian forces had already suffered many losses because disease was rife and food was scarce. One of those lost was Sybil, Queen of Jerusalem.

Louis arrived at Acre in April and Richard arrived in June. The city surrendered on 12 July and Philip then returned to France, possibly because of illness. Richard was now in charge. He set off south to Jerusalem, fighting the only pitched battle against Saladin during the journey. The battle, at Arsuf, was decisively won by Richard, who demonstrated his military genius and proved that he truly deserved his title of "Lionheart". Richard then went on to secure Jaffa and control of the coast. However, the ultimate goal of Jerusalem was never to be his. Richard knew that, even if Jerusalem were taken, it could never be held, so he did not lay siege to the city, although his army got to within sight of it twice. The disappointment of not taking Jerusalem led many of the crusaders to leave for home. Added to that, Richard received word that his European lands were threatened by Philip II of France. Saladin also had troubles to contend with, including an army that was going hungry and was reluctant to fight. Therefore, on 2 September, Saladin and Richard agreed a truce. The Christians kept the coast from Jaffa to Tyre, but Ascalon was to be returned to Saladin once the Christians had painstakingly removed their fortifications there. Christian pilgrims would be allowed free passage into Jerusalem.

Although the crusaders failed to take Jerusalem, the Third Crusade can be considered a success. Richard had managed to take back some crusader lands and had stabilized the area, the truce between the two sides holding until the start of the Fourth Crusade.

It was at the start of the thirteenth century that the Fourth Crusade set out for Jerusalem, but this crusade would never come close to its holy goal. Transport and provisions had been arranged with the Venetians ahead of the crusade. However, once the army was formed it was found to be much smaller than anticipated. The Venetians had, therefore, been contracted to supply too much and the crusaders could not pay. A deal was struck whereby the crusaders would take the city of Zara, which had rebelled against Venice, and the Venetians would hold off taking payment until the crusaders could pay from booty taken once they had reached Muslim territory. Zara was a Christian city and the pope did not consent to the plan. He was, however, ignored and the invasion successfully went ahead in November 1202.

The crusaders still did not go straight to the Holy Land from Zara. Instead they got caught up in the internal politics of the Byzantine Empire. For a large sum of money, which was much needed for the crusade, they agreed to topple the existing emperor for another contender to the throne. Therefore, in June 1203 they arrived in Constantinople and Alexius III was deposed for Alexius IV and his father. However, their reign was not to last and a coup removed the new emperor in January 1204. This left the crusaders not fully paid and with no prospect of seeing the money owed. They declared war on Constantinople and in April 1204 the city fell. The sacking that followed will go down in history as a truly despicable act. The crusaders raped and pillaged the city for three days. They took as booty everything they could carry, including holy relics from the many churches they defiled. Everything else they destroyed; centuries worth of exquisite art, architecture and knowledge, all destroyed in a matter of days.

The booty was split between the crusaders and Venice. Much of the empire was also split between the victors. Although Pope Innocent III was against the crusaders attacking Constantinople, once it was done, he hoped that the Churches of the east and west could be united. However, because of the resentment and betrayal felt by the people of the Eastern Empire towards the invaders, this was not to be. The sack of Constantinople would be the final nail in the coffin for any kind of reconciliation between the churches of the east and west.

There were a number of further crusades to the Muslim east. However, the Third Crusade was to be the last crusade to have any lasting effect. In the thirteenth century a string of absentee, ineffectual rulers and internal conflicts had left the crusader states weak. Eventually, castle by castle, city by city, they were lost

and in 1291 Acre, the final mainland crusader stronghold in the Levant, fell to the Egyptian Mamluks. After two centuries of conflict and bloodshed the crusader states of the Holy Land were no more.

Later Crusades

The Holy Land crusades were not the only holy wars waged by the Christians in the Middle Ages. In Europe itself, throughout most of the Middle Ages, there had been a long-standing conflict between Christian and Muslim. The Muslim Moors had taken most of the Iberian Peninsula in the eighth century. Not long after, the Christians fought to reclaim the land taken and so the Reconquista, meaning "reconquest", began.

However, until the eleventh century the Reconquista lacked drive. Even though there were a number of clashes and some of the northern territories were retaken by the Christians, quite often Muslim, Christian and Jew lived side by side in relative peace.

That was to change in the first half of the eleventh century as Muslim unity fragmented and a number of separate Muslim states were formed. Around the same time, the crusading spirit took hold of the Christians in the north and they started a serious offensive against the Moors. As the Muslim states were occupied with troubles among themselves, their resistance was weak. In 1085 Christian forces took the strategically important city of Toledo, which led to the arrival of the Almohads from North Africa. These fundamental Muslims united the Muslims again. However, they were intolerant of other religions and so went on the offensive, rather than taking just a defensive stand.

ABOVE Cathay and the Empire of the Great Khan, from a map by Fra Mauro Camaldolese, 1459.

In 1212 the war between the Almohads and Christian forces came to a head in the Battle of Las Navas de Tolosa in the Sierra Morena in the south of Spain. A massive Christian force, which included kings from the Christian states in the peninsula, knights from the military order and thousands upon thousands of crusaders, defeated the Almohads. In the following decades their main strongholds were conquered by the Christian kings: Valencia and Majorca fell to James I of Aragon; Cordoba, Alicante and Seville were taken by Ferdinand III of Castile and Badajoz was conquered by Alfonso IX of Leon. This forced the remaining Muslims into the area around Granada, where the Emirate of Granada was their last remaining foothold on the peninsula.

Thus, by the middle of the thirteenth century the Muslims had lost control of most of the peninsula, holding only the small enclave in the south of Spain around the city of Granada. Around the same time, in 1249, the Reconquista in Portugal was concluded successfully. The Portuguese Christians had been aided during the twelfth century by Holy Land crusaders, who had broken their sea journey during both the Second and Third Crusades to assist in the battle against the Moors.

It was not until the fifteenth century that Granada would be successfully challenged. In 1469 Isabella I of Castile married Ferdinand II of Aragon. Their union joined together the kingdom of Spain under one mantle, making it strong enough to take on the final Muslim stronghold. In 1492 Granada surrendered to the Christians. Moorish rule in Spain was finally over after 800 years. Isabella and Ferdinand then ordered the conversion to Christianity of all Jews. Those who did not convert were expelled from Spain. Ten years later the same rule was applied to the Muslims. Spain was now a completely Christian country.

The Wendish Crusade

The Wends were Slavic tribes that had settled in Germany between the Elbe and Oder Rivers. During the Early Middle Ages they fought against the Franks and Saxons, whose lands they bordered. The Franks, under Charlemagne, wished to convert them to Christianity and the Saxons wished to expand their empire. However, the Wends maintained the upper hand and by the end of the tenth century they were still pagan and had reversed much of previous Saxon incursions.

By the middle of the twelfth century, though, their position had become precarious. Their Christian neighbours were gaining strength and, in 1143, neighbouring states seized parts of their territory. Then in 1147 Bernard de Clairvaux recruited in Germany for the Second Crusade (see page 131). Rather than go to the Holy Land, the Saxons were keen to fight the pagan Wends. Pope Eugenius III pronounced that such a fight would be considered a crusade and so the Wendish Crusade began. The force against the Wends mainly comprised Saxons and Danes. They attacked that year, killing many. A number of Wends did convert to Christianity, though they soon reverted to their pagan ways once the enemy armies were gone. In all, as a crusade to convert a pagan people, the military exercise was not a success. However, it did pave the way for the future conversion of the Wends and colonization of their lands.

The Wendish Crusade also paved the way for other crusades against pagans, especially in the Balkans. In 1171 Pope Alexander III stated that going on crusade against the pagans of the north would offer the same indulgences as going on a Holy Land crusade. In the decades that followed a number of crusades were declared against various peoples of the north and the Teutonic Knights, a German religious military order, played a major part in conquering pagan territories in the Baltic. The Livonian Crusade lasted almost one hundred years and by 1290 saw the subjugation of the pagan tribes living on the eastern shores of the Baltic. In Prussia, during the thirteenth century, the Teutonic Knights assisted in conquering the Prussians. By the end of the century they were victorious and the local tribes were forcibly converted to Christianity.

The Albigensian Crusade

Also known as the Cathar Crusade, the Albigensian Crusade commenced in 1209. Its target was the Cathars, a Christian sect based mainly in the Languedoc region of southern France. In previous decades a number of attempts had been made to try to make the heretical Cathars see the error of their ways. Preachers such as Saint Dominic, who founded the Dominican order in reaction to the heresy of the Cathars, were sent to the area, but to no avail. One of the main problems with

rooting out the heresy was that the nobles of the area, who should have been repressing it, were often tolerant of the Cathars. Raymond VI of Toulouse was one of these nobles.

In 1208 Raymond was excommunicated for his support of the Cathars. Then, soon afterwards, a papal legate was murdered after having a very unpleasant meeting with Raymond. It was this murder that led Pope Innocent III to finally instigate a crusade again the Cathars. After years of preaching to deaf ears, he had decided that force was the only way to deal with the heretics.

In 1209 the crusade set forth to rid the land of heretics. One of the crusaders was none other than Raymond VI, who had made peace with the Church, most probably more for reasons of self-interest than religious conviction. The first town to be taken was Béziers. This was home to both Catholic and Cathar, yet the crusaders slaughtered almost the whole population. Allegedly, the papal legate responsible for the massacre had stated "Kill them all. God will know his own" in response to the question of how to distinguish heretic from Christian.

When word of the massacre got out, many towns and villages surrendered to the crusaders rather than suffer the same fate. Although some, such as Carcassonne, held

out for a short time they too were taken. Around this time Simon de Montfort became leader of the crusade. Under his leadership the crusaders took town after town, converting and killing as they went. In 1211 Raymond VI was excommunicated again and he fled to England. In 1215 his lands, including Toulouse, were given to Simon de Montfort. Most of the Cathar lands were now in the hands of the crusaders. That year the indulgence given to crusaders against the Cathars was rescinded because the Pope wished to launch another crusade to the east.

Raymond returned from England and a rebellion was started. In 1217 he retook Toulouse, which was then besieged by de Montfort, who was killed during the siege. Much of the territory previously taken by the crusaders was taken back by Raymond. Then in 1225 another crusade was called against the Cathars. This one was led by King Louis VIII of France. He was successful, but died in 1226 before the completion of the crusade. It was his wife Blanche of Castile who, as Queen Regent, eventually ended the conflict by agreeing a treaty with Raymond VI's son, Raymond VII. The treaty was almost completely in favour of the French crown who, under its terms, would eventually own all of Raymond's ancestral lands.

Although the two decades of bloody fighting had not managed to completely suppress the Cathars in Languedoc, it resulted in an inquisition that systematically rooted out the remaining heretics. By the end of the fourteenth century the Cathars had been all but eliminated from the area.

A number of other, smaller, crusades took place during the Middle Ages. Some of these, such as the Crusade of Nicopolis, were aimed at stemming the tide of Ottoman expansion. Others, such as the Hussite Crusade, were against other Christian movements declared heretical by the Roman Catholic Church. However, by the end of the sixteenth century, with the advent of the Protestant Church greatly diminishing their appeal, the crusades ceased altogether.

The Medieval Inquisition

In 1184 Pope Lucius III instigated the episcopal inquisition in response to the growing number of heretical movements. Local bishops were supposed to instigate inquisitions in their dioceses. However, there was no central control of these and no uniformity. In 1227, as a result of the Albigensian Crusade, Pope Gregory IX instigated a papal inquisition to deal with the issue of heresy. The inquisitors were mainly friars from the recently formed Dominican and Franciscan orders.

In the late 1240s guidelines were given for the running of inquisitions and in 1252 Pope Innocent IV issued the Ad extirpanda papal bull, officially sanctioning the use of torture during inquisitions. However, there were limits to the extent of the torture used as, among other things, loss of life through torture was not deemed acceptable. Punishments depended on a number of factors, including confession, recantation and the naming of other heretics. Punishments could range from loss of property or imprisonment to public recantation and banishment. The worst offenders would be handed over to secular authorities to be burnt at the stake.

Military Tactics and Weapons

During the Middle Ages numerous wars were fought between a hugely diverse array of combatants. Tactics and weaponry varied widely depending on such things as the terrain being fought over and the culture, wealth and skill of the soldiers involved. While for some, such as the Mongols, mobility was key, for others using tightly grouped infantrymen was the preferred tactic on the battlefield.

Light cavalry, including the mounted archers of the east, had been used in warfare for centuries. However, the medieval period saw the development of heavy cavalry. Armoured knights would use shock tactics on the battlefield to charge enemy lines and crush the enemy infantry. These formidable troops would use their lances to dislodge opposition, sending those hit flying into their fellow soldiers. Once the wave of lance attacks was over, the mounted knights would use any of a number of weapons, such as maces or swords to continue the fight. However, these tactics could only be used in the right environment, so knights would often find themselves fighting on foot during a battle since many terrains were not conducive to cavalry charges. The horses would be kept behind the lines and used for chasing down the enemy at the end of the battle.

During the Late Middle Ages infantry tactics were developed to counter the heavy cavalry charges. Pikes

BELOW A 15th-century crossbow, jack and crossbow darts. The crossbow was one of the most popular weapons of the Middle Ages, most probably as it did not take a lot of strength to use and the bolt it fired was capable of penetrating armour. Due to its lethality, it was outlawed by the Church for use against Christians.

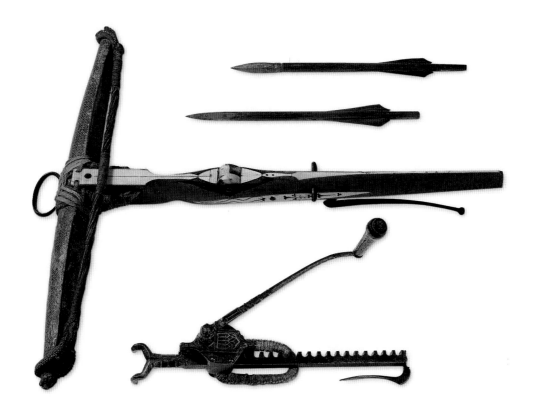

were used by a number of armies, such as the Swiss and Scots, because a cavalry charge against a wall of spears would often result in serious injury for the horsemen. During the Hundred Years' War, the English used longbowmen to rain arrows down on the charging knights. Perhaps the most famous use of the longbow was at the Battle of Agincourt in 1415, where the French were routed by the English, in no small part thanks to the skill of the longbowmen.

Pitched battles were not the only type of warfare undertaken. The period saw the construction of a large number of castles and fortifications. As the taking of an enemy's power base was instrumental to most campaigns, siege warfare was prevalent during this time and a variety of weapons and tactics were used to breach enemy walls. Weapons used by the besiegers included the battering ram; the mangonel – a catapult that could

send a large number of projectiles, such as rocks, hurtling at the enemy; the ballista – a kind of large crossbow; the trebuchet – a counterweighted catapult that could throw huge missiles at high speed; and the siege tower – a tower on wheels that would protect the ladders of those trying to scale the walls of the fortification.

During a siege the tactics used by the besieging army would often be as instrumental in winning the siege as the siege weapons. Undermining was common. A tunnel would be dug under a part of the castle wall and wooden supports would be used as shoring. Once the tunnel was complete, it would be set on fire, burning the props to collapse the tunnel. This would cause the wall above to fall, compromising the stuctural integrity of the castle. Another favoured tactic was treachery. A traitor within the castle or town walls could shorten a siege considerably by methods such as opening gates

for besieging troops or passing on tactical information. Siege warfare was to take a new turn in the Late Middle Ages, with the arrival of gunpowder and cannon. Walls that once stood strong against all attacks crumbled under the onslaught of this new weapon, so the designs of fortifications were adapted to take account of the new foe.

One of the most vital aspects of any war was logistics. If the supply chain failed, then more often than not, the battle was lost. An invading army could sometimes decide instead to commandeer provisions along the way. However, this tactic could backfire dramatically – as happened during the first crusade. The Turks had followed a scorched-earth policy and destroyed everything as they retreated. This left crusader armies on the brink of starvation and, therefore, much weakened. Before the Battle of Hattin, Saladin cut the Christian army off from any water supply, forcing them to face his army parched under the blazing sun. It comes as no surprise that the crusader army suffered a staggering defeat as a result of this very effective tactic.

One of the most effective weapons of the Byzantine Empire was Greek Fire. Invented during the seventh century, it was a flammable liquid that, once ignited, could not be extinguished by water. It would often be used during naval battles, where it could be launched out of tubes located on the Byzantine ships. Greek fire was a significant factor in numerous Byzantine victories because it often gave the Byzantine forces the upper hand in battle. The exact composition and delivery of the mixture were so secret that they were never discovered by the enemies of the empire, although attempts were made to copy them. To this day no-one has worked out the precise ingredients of Greek fire.

The Mongols

During the High Middle Ages the Europeans and Muslims were not the only ones with dreams of conquest and expansion. To the east a terrifying new power was gathering force. When unleashed, this force spread like wildfire, leaving despair and devastation in its wake.

In Central Asia, Turkish and Mongol nomadic tribes had been dominant for centuries. Towards the end of the twelfth century a Mongolian warrior by the name of Temujin started to unite many of the different tribes into one force under his leadership. In 1206 he was declared khan ("ruler") and gave himself the name Genghis Khan ("supreme ruler"). He then started his military campaigns of conquest. In his 20-year reign he extended the Mongol Empire into Russia in one direction and China in another. By the time of his death in 1227 the Mongols controlled a huge expanse of land in Asia from the Caspian Sea to the China Sea.

The reason for the Mongols' staggering military success was simple. They fielded armies of light cavalry consisting of mounted archers who used their mobility and speed to weaken the enemy. The light cavalry would then be followed by heavier cavalry, armoured mounted lancers, who would swiftly dispatch those who survived the archers' attack. The Mongols were also highly trained and disciplined – in stark contrast to the mainly peasant armies that they often faced. Added to that, they fought with a terrifying ruthlessness. In many of the towns and cities the Mongols captured after resistance, the streets ran red with the blood of the slain. This reputation for brutality stood the Mongols in good stead, as some towns would simply surrender in the hope of being spared.

Although the Mongols often left mass destruction behind them, they were also empire builders. They built roads and established an immense trade network. They took control of the Silk Road, an ancient trading route that had linked China with the Roman Empire, keeping it free from bandits. Along various trade routes they established a system of post houses where traders could stay overnight in safety and be fed, and messengers could change their horses or pass the post on to the next messenger. The Mongols had a very relaxed attitude to different religions, so those people absorbed into their empire could usually practise their own religion without fear of persecution. They also had very strict laws and harsh punishments for those who did not follow their rules.

On Genghis' death, the empire was split among his four sons, with his son, Ögödei, becoming Great Khan. The Mongols continued the expansion of their empire under Ögödei, invading Poland and Hungary in eastern Europe. Ögödei died in 1241 and the Mongol armies, rather than carrying on the invasion of Europe, returned to the east. In 1251, after years of power struggles, Möngke Khan, one of Genghis' grandsons, became the Great Khan. He

was followed by his brother, Kublai Khan, in 1260. Kublai was responsible for completing the invasion of China and founded the Yuan dynasty there, which survived until 1368, when it was overthrown and supplanted by the Chinese Ming dynasty.

The Mongols did not only conquer huge areas of Asia. They were also responsible for the invasion and destruction of the Islamic lands of the Caliphate. In 1258 the Mongols sacked Baghdad, killing the last Abbasid caliph. The sack of Baghdad was one of history's great atrocities. The Mongols looted and destroyed everything they could see. The House of Wisdom, an important centre of learning, was destroyed along with its contents, great buildings were razed to the ground and, although estimates vary, it is thought that at least 200,000 people were killed. Some accounts state that as many as a million people perished in the slaughter. Baghdad was left a desecrated ruin that would take centuries to return to even a semblance of its former glory.

The Mongols were finally stopped in the Middle East by the Mamluks of Egypt. However, by that time the Mongols had added territory to their empire that encompassed modern-day Iran, Iraq, Syria, and parts of Turkey. The Mongol Empire did not last, though. Feuding between the khans, added to the difficulties of ruling such a far-reaching empire, took its toll and by the end of the fourteenth century Mongol unity was no more. The vast empire build up by the Mongols fractured into a number of smaller states, many of which were themselves conquered by other nations.

Wars in Wales and Scotland

Back in Europe, in 1272 Henry III, John I's son, died and his son became Edward I of England. Henry had spent much of his reign preoccupied with internal affairs, especially baronial discontent within his realm. Although by Edward's succession the barons had been mostly dealt with, he spent the early years of his reign addressing internal matters, especially legal reform. However, he was soon embroiled with his nearest neighbours – the Welsh and the Scots.

During Henry III's reign, Llywelyn ap Gruffudd, Prince of Gwynedd, had expanded his territory. Henry, preoccupied with the barons, had agreed to the Treaty

of Montgomery in 1267, which, in return for homage, allowed Llywelyn to keep land he had taken and officially recognized him as Prince of Wales. When Edward came to the throne, he wished to curb Llywelyn's power. Therefore, using Llywelyn's refusal to declare fealty to him as an excuse, Edward invaded Wales in 1277. The war was short-lived because Llywelyn realized that he could not win. He surrendered and Edward stripped him of all his lands apart from Gwynedd. Llywelyn was, however, allowed to keep the title of Prince of Wales.

In 1282 the Welsh, unhappy with Edward's rule, rebelled. Llywelyn and his younger brother, Dafydd, were at the forefront of the rebellion. The rebellion was soon put down and Llywelyn was killed in battle in December 1282 and Dafydd captured and executed in 1283. Edward then continued his programme of

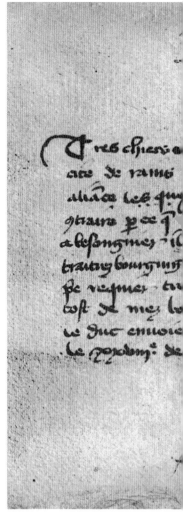

castle-building, which he had begun after Llywelyn's first defeat. The massive structures rose up throughout Wales as symbols of English dominance. Edward's son, the future Edward II, was born in the incomplete castle at Caernarfon in 1284 and he was invested with the title Prince of Wales, a title still used by the heir to the English throne today. Further rebellions in 1287 and 1294–5 were also put down. Edward's subjugation of the Welsh was so complete that there were no further uprisings until the fifteenth century, when Owain Glyndŵr led the last great Welsh rebellion.

Although England had long had a troubled history with Wales, relations with Scotland were good when Edward came to power. However, in 1290 this was to change. The King of Scotland, Alexander III, had died in an accident in 1286 and his heiress, his young granddaughter Margaret, had died in 1290. Margaret had been destined to marry Edward's heir. However, with her death the succession to the crown of Scotland was in no way clear cut. There were a number of claimants to the throne and Edward agreed to decide upon the best claimant. Edward considered Scotland to be a fief of the English crown and he wished to enforce Scottish recognition of his position as overlord and to assert his authority over the Scots.

He chose John Balliol as the rightful heir of the throne. Balliol duly paid homage to Edward and was crowned

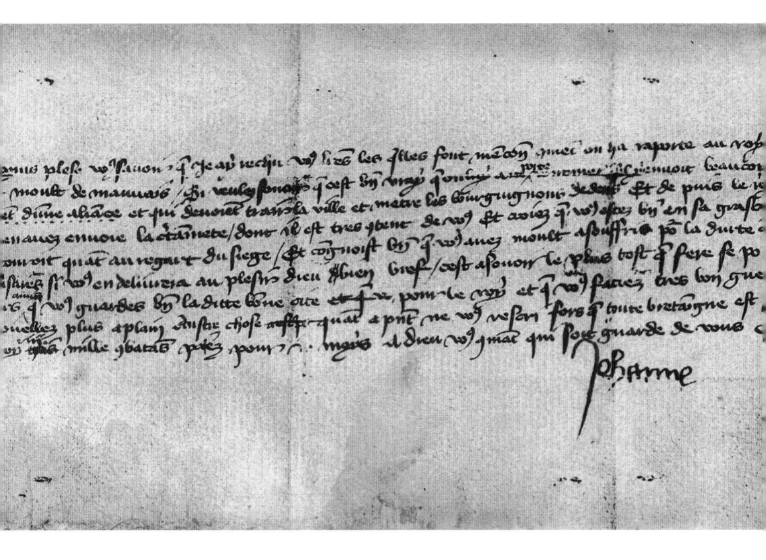

Johanne

king. However, the Scots were resistant to Edward's efforts to enforce his authority. In 1295 they allied with France, then at war with England. Edward retaliated by marching on Scotland in 1296. He crushed Scottish resistance, deposed Balliol and sent him to the Tower. He then set up his own government of the country. However, it was to be a short victory for Edward. In 1297 the Scots, under the leadership of William Wallace and Andrew Moray, rebelled. The rebels were successful at the Battle of Stirling Bridge in September, but they were defeated in July at the Battle of Falkirk. In the years following this victory Edward continued his subjugation of Scotland and in 1305 again installed his own government there.

Wallace was eventually arrested by the English in 1305 and executed as a traitor in London.

However, despite appearances to the contrary, Scotland was not beaten. In 1306 Robert the Bruce had himself crowned as king and went to war with the English. Although Edward died in 1307, the war with Scotland carried on during the reign of his son, Edward II. In 1314 Edward II marched on Scotland, but was soundly defeated by the Scots under Robert the Bruce at the Battle of Bannockburn. In 1328, the year after Edward II's death, the Treaty of Northampton, which recognized Scotland's independence, was signed. That was not to be the end of the war with England, as the

RIGHT The amazing story of Joan of Arc is so incredible that it could be fiction. She was a pious, illiterate, 17-year-old peasant girl from a small French village, yet she was given command of an army and led it to its victory. Here she is depicted in *Vie des Femmes Célèbres*, c. 1505.

struggles between the two countries disintegrated into a series of raids, invasions and occupations that would carry on for decades.

The Hundred Years' War

Only a few years after the Treaty of Northampton was signed, the Hundred Years' War began. The was actually a series of wars between the English and the French that lasted from 1337 to 1453. Before 1337 England and France had already been at odds over control of the English fief of Gascony, in France. The French wished to execute more authority over this hugely prosperous region, so disputes with the English over issues such as borders and the rights of inhabitants had been going on for decades. However, it is possible that this disagreement would never have become all-out war had it not been for two other factors.

The first factor was the line of succession to the French throne. In less than 15 years four kings of France – Philip IV and his three sons – died. Edward III of England was the next in line for the throne through his mother Isabella, who was Philip IV's daughter. However, in 1328 the French crowned Philip VI, who was from a cadet branch of the Capetian dynasty. This was later justified by citing Salic law, which stated that the crown could be inherited only down the male line, so descendants through females could not succeed to the throne.

The second factor was the alliance between France and Scotland. In 1333 England was again at war with Scotland. The French supported the Scots, so when the Scottish king, David II, was forced to flee, he escaped to the safety of France. Things came to a head in 1337, when King Philip confiscated the region of Gascony. Edward had not pressed his claim to the throne in 1328 but, with this new development, he claimed the throne of France as rightfully his and declared war.

Gascony was invaded by the French and the French fleet raided the English coast at will. In 1339 Edward finally invaded France and a number of raids ensued. However, when Philip's much larger French army approached, Edward retreated. The naval situation was to come to a head in 1340 at the Battle of Sluys. The English and French fleets faced each other at the entrance of Sluys Harbour, in the southwest of the Netherlands. The English annihilated the French fleet, leaving the English in control of the Channel. However, although Edward had the advantage at sea, he was not able to press this advantage on land, so a truce was signed in September 1340.

From 1342 there were a number of skirmishes and confrontations, but no major confrontations. The English used the tactic of intermittently raiding the French countryside, systematically pillaging villages and towns, destabilizing local economies, destroying civilian morale and keeping the French on the defensive. This type of harassment continued throughout the war, devastating large parts of the French countryside.

In July 1346 Edward III and his son, Edward of Woodstock, Prince of Wales, later known as the Black Prince, landed in Normandy with a large army. The English plundered their way through Normandy, leaving a wave of destruction in their wake, until August, when the French confronted them at Crécy. The English found themselves facing a much larger French army, led by Philip VI. Despite the inequality in numbers, the English were victorious, mainly as a result of the skill of their archers, and the French were routed. Wounded, Philip retreated from the battlefield and the English made

their way towards Calais. Calais was besieged and surrendered in August 1347. However, Edward agreed a truce in September 1347, most likely because of a lack of the funds necessary to continue.

During the following year the Plague devastated the populations of both France and England (see pages 62–63). Although the war continued, it was on a small scale. Then, in 1356 Edward, Prince of Wales, invaded France again. He met the French army at Poitiers in September. The ensuing battle was a resounding victory for the English. John II of France, who had succeeded his father Philip VI in 1350, was captured and a huge ransom was demanded for his return. The Treaty of Brétigny was finally agreed in 1360. By the terms of this treaty Edward renounced any claim to the throne of France and was given sovereignty over the whole of Aquitaine and various other French lands in return. However, John II died in captivity in 1364 and his son, Charles V, resumed hostilities in 1369. The French forced the English back, taking much of their territory. Edward, Prince of Wales, died in 1376 and his father died shortly afterwards in 1377. In 1380 Charles V of France also died. These deaths, along with both sides being preoccupied with internal affairs, led to a time of relative peace. However, this was not to last.

Resumption and End of the Hundred Years' War

In France after the death of Charles V his son, Charles VI, succeeded to the throne. However, the new king suffered from bouts of madness, which made him unfit to rule for months at a time. This left his uncles, Philip, Duke of Burgundy, and Louis, Duke of Orléans, vying for power. The ensuing power struggles saw the Duke of Orléans murdered and parts of France embroiled in civil conflict between the Armagnacs, who backed Orléans, and the Burgundians.

Meanwhile, England was also not free from the power games of the nobles. In 1399 Richard II, Edward III's grandson, was deposed in favour of Henry Bolingbroke, Richard's cousin, who became Henry IV. Henry's reign was fraught with violence as he put down rebellions from within his realm and dealt with threats from without. He was successful and when his son, Henry V, succeeded him in 1413 he gained a relatively peaceful realm.

Henry V, with most internal disputes having been dealt with by his father, could turn the attention of the English crown back to France. In August 1415 Henry invaded France. He landed at the town of Harfleur in Normandy, which he captured. From there, using the destructive raiding tactics of previous English armies, he marched towards Calais. On the way, in October, he was met by a large French army near the village of Agincourt. The English army was exhausted, depleted as a result of disease and running low on supplies. The French, on the other hand, fielded a much larger, less rundown, army which included many mounted knights. Despite the inequality between the armies, the terrain of the battlefield and superior English tactics – longbowmen were again used to great effect – meant that the English were victorious. English casualties are thought to have numbered in the hundreds, while thousands of Frenchmen lost their lives.

As a result of the battle Henry returned to England a hero. France was left weakened, with a large number of the governing class dead and the conflict between the Armagnacs and Burgundians renewed. Seeing an opportunity to take advantage of the internal strife in France to press his claim for the French crown, Henry formally allied himself with the Burgundians in 1419, after John, Duke of Burgundy, was assassinated by the Armagnacs. This union was to prove essential to English success. In 1420 the Treaty of Troyes was agreed between Henry V and Charles VI. The terms stated that Henry would marry Charles' daughter, Catherine, and become the heir to the French throne. The dauphin, Charles' son, was, therefore, disinherited. Henry did not long enjoy his success, as he predeceased Charles by a couple of months in 1422.

At the time both kings died, the north of France was controlled by the English and Burgundians and most of the south of France was loyal to the dauphin. Henry was succeeded by his infant son, Henry VI, whose regents claimed the thrones of both France and England as his, as per the terms of the 1420 treaty. The dauphin also claimed the throne as his and was supported by the Armagnacs in his claim. The war, therefore, carried on.

In September 1428 the English began besieging the strategically important city of Orléans. As the English lacked the strength to attack the town immediately, the siege dragged on. In February 1429 a young peasant girl had an audience with the dauphin at his court at Chinon. Claiming to have heard voices telling her to drive the English out of France, she wished to lead the army. The dauphin, most probably desperate by this time, acceded to her wishes and Joan of Arc arrived at Orléans in April.

What followed was nothing short of miraculous. Joan rallied the French troops and, under her influence, they broke the siege at Orléans. She led the army to a number of further victories, including the Battle of Patay on 18 June 1429, where the English were decimated. These victories allowed the French to march on Rheims, where the dauphin would be crowned King Charles VII. In 1430 Joan was captured by the Burgundians. They sold her to the English who put her on trial, found her guilty of heresy and burned her at the stake. She was found innocent 25 years later at a retrial.

After the defeat at Patay Franco-English alliances began to disintegrate and in 1435 the Burgundians changed sides. The French forces carried on with their mission to conquer all English-held lands in France. The war finally ended in 1453 with the Battle of Castillon, which returned the last remaining English areas of Aquitaine to France. All that was left to the English of their once vast French holdings was Calais, which they held until 1558.

The Wars of the Roses

The end of the Hundred Years' War did not signal peace for England. While on the Continent matters had been seemingly resolved, at home trouble was just beginning. Henry VI was a weak and unstable king. He had apparently inherited his grandfather Charles VI's malaise and suffered frequent bouts of madness during his reign. This led to England being controlled by various power-hungry ministers.

Their disastrous rule led, in no small part, to the defeat of the English in France, to high taxes, corruption, and a country that had descended into civil discontent and lawlessness. This was to be the backdrop for the start of the dynastic struggle between the royal houses of York and Lancaster, which came to be called the Wars of the Roses.

In 1453 Henry had a serious lapse into insanity and his cousin, Richard Duke of York, was made Lord

Protector while Henry was incapacitated. When Henry recovered in 1455 he again came under the influence of his ministers and domineering queen, Margaret of Anjou. Richard and his supporters were removed from government shortly after Henry's recovery. This led to Richard taking up arms, probably for self-protection as much as anything else, and marching on London.

The first battle of the war was at St Albans on 22 May 1455. The Yorkists under Richard beat Henry's Lancastrian forces. After the battle an uneasy truce was enacted and Richard again became Lord Protector, while Henry was absent again. However, once again Henry recovered and, under the influence of his wife, removed Richard from office. The war resumed in 1459, with the Lancastrian forces being beaten at the Battle of Northampton in July 1460. Henry was captured during the battle, which led to an agreement between the parties that Richard would become his heir.

The war did not end there. In December 1460 Richard was killed by Queen Margaret's forces at the Battle of Wakefield. This meant that Richard's 18-year-old son, Edward, was now Duke of York and the war carried on. In February 1461 the Lancastrians claimed another victory, this time against the Yorkist Earl of Warwick, at St Albans. They also retook Henry, who had been captured the previous year. While this was happening Edward Duke of York was making his way to London, beating the Lancastrians at Mortimer's Cross on 2 February 1461 along the way. Edward was crowned king on 4 March and he then marched north in pursuit of Henry and his army.

The two armies met at Towton on 29 March to fight what would be the bloodiest battle of the wars. The battle raged for many hours in a blizzard. When it was over, with the Yorkists claiming victory, the battlefield and surrounding area were strewn with thousands dead and dying. Some estimate that there were more than 20,000 casualties that day, many of whom were brutally cut down as they retreated. Henry fled to Scotland. However, even this did not signal the end of the war. The war resumed again in 1469 and in 1470 Edward was deposed and Henry VI was restored to the throne.

Edward escaped to the Netherlands, from whence he returned in March 1471. He met forces of the Earl of Warwick at the Battle of Barnet on 14 April 1471. In the ensuing clash Warwick was killed and Edward was victorious. In May the forces of Queen Margaret were confronted in the battle of Tewksbury, during which her son, Edward, was killed. Henry VI was killed in the Tower of London shortly after the battle, leaving no direct heirs for the throne.

Edward IV ruled until his sudden death in 1483. He was succeeded by his son, Edward V, who was only 13 at the time, making him vulnerable to political intrigue. Edward IV's brother, Richard Duke of Gloucester, usurped the throne to become Richard III and put Edward and his younger brother in the Tower of London. The two boys, who have gone down in history as the tragic "Princes in the Tower", disappeared shortly afterwards, presumed murdered by Richard. Richard was not to reign for long. In 1485 another Lancastrian claimant to the throne, Henry Tudor, invaded England. Richard III was killed at the ensuing Battle of Bosworth Field on 22 August 1485. Henry was crowned King Henry VII. He married the heir to the House of York, Elizabeth of York, joining the houses of York and Lancaster and ending the 30-year conflict.

The end of the Wars of the Roses heralded the start of a vibrant new age; an age of reformation, political machination and conflict; an age ruled by perhaps the most famous dynasty of them all – the Tudors.

OPPOSITE
Richard III at the Battle of Bosworth, where the House of Lancaster finally prevailed over the House of York.

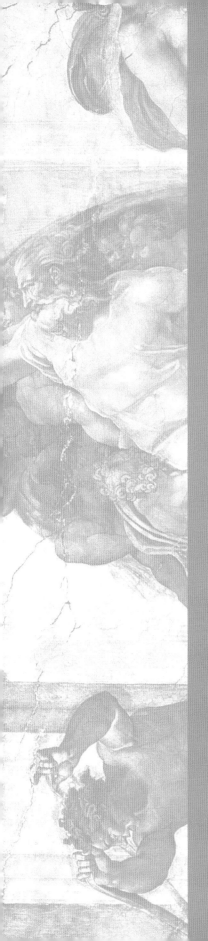

CHAPTER

6

"THE NOBLEST PLEASURE
IS THE JOY OF
UNDERSTANDING."

LEONARDO DA VINCI (1452–1519)

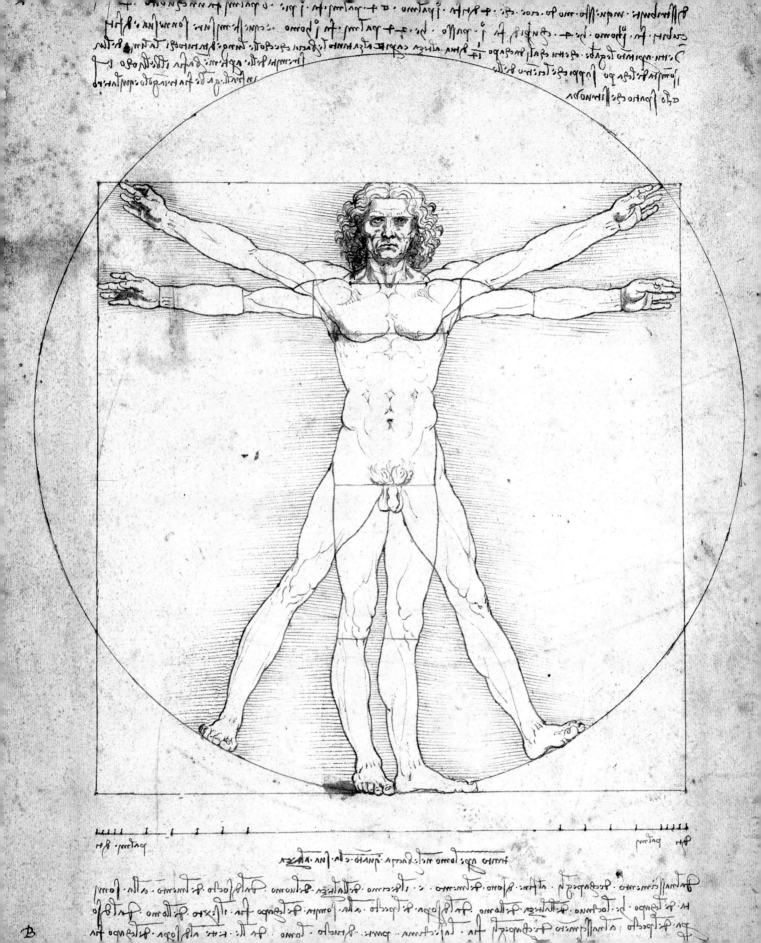

THE DAWN OF A NEW AGE

Conclusion

The Middle Ages have often been portrayed as a dark era marked by ignorance, conflict, intolerance and lack of innovation. However, from the creation of the simple horse collar to the vast trading networks of the Mongols and the seminal invention of the printing press, this complex time saw developments that would affect the world for centuries to come. Ultimately, it paved the way for the Renaissance period that followed.

This age of discovery and exploration saw an explosion of culture and science across Europe and beyond. Explorers such as Christopher Columbus and Vasco de Gama discovered rich, new worlds, leading to European colonization of many of these new lands. Explorers brought back untold riches from their travels, adding to the wealth and prosperity of their patrons.

In the field of science huge advances were made. Gallileo Galilei, Isaac Newton and Nicolaus Copernicus are just a few of the scientists whose theories are still in use to this day. Perhaps the most famous of all the great Renaissance minds, Leonardo da Vinci, led the way with his seemingly unquenchable quest for knowledge. Artist, architect and engineer, among many other professions, he was responsible for some of the most influential paintings of his time – his *Mona Lisa* is perhaps the most famous painting in the world. Using his scientific intellect and artistic talent, he was responsible for drawings such as the Vitruvian man. The Vitruvian man illustrated the proportions of the human body, showing how each individual part of the body was simply a fraction of the whole. Leonardo and the Roman architect Marco Vitruvius Pollio, after whom the drawing was named, both believed that these proportions should be used in architecture.

Leonardo da Vinci was but one of a number of magnificent artists, architects and sculptors who emerged during the Renaissance. Michelangelo di Lodovico Buonarroti Simoni, Donato di Niccolò di Betto Bardi and Raffaello Sanzio da Urbino (better known as Michaelangelo, Donatello and Raphael) are all names that are synonymous with the era. Michelangelo's painting of the Sistine Chapel in the Vatican is still awe-inspiring and Donatello's incredible sculptures still stand in Italian cities such as Padua and Florence.

The arts and science were not the only fields to flourish during the Renaissance. In no small part because of the advances in science and technology, medical knowledge also improved. Medical texts became more accessible, thanks to the advent of the printing press in the late Middle Ages. Works such as *De humani corporis fabrica*, by the anatomist Andreas Vesalius, corrected errors made by earlier physicians, such as Galen of Pergamon and gave a much more accurate view of the human body.

Although the Renaissance is considered a period of enlightenment, the centuries following the Middle Ages

were still marred by religious intolerance and ignorance. In Spain the infamous Spanish Inquisition was instigated by Queen Isabella and King Ferdinand and is thought to have been responsible for the deaths of thousands of alleged heretics, many of whom were probably innocent. In Europe there was a resurgence in the number of accusations of witchcraft and witch hunts. The number of witch trials rose dramatically and it is believed that across Europe at least 50,000 people were executed for witchcraft in just a few centuries.

The Middle Ages not only opened the door to the Renaissance, they also saw the fabric of Europe change completely. What was once a continent ruled in great part by pagan barbarians had become a number of Christian states, each with its own distinctive character and powerful ruler. The foundations for modern day Europe had been laid.

INDEX

Page 75: The Dictatus Papae

1. That the Roman church was founded by God alone.
2. That the Roman pontiff alone can with right be called universal.
3. That he alone can depose or reinstate bishops.
4. That, in a council his legate, even if a lower grade, is above all bishops, and can pass sentence of deposition against them.
5. That the pope may depose the absent.
6. That, among other things, we ought not to remain in the same house with those excommunicated by him.
7. That for him alone is it lawful, according to the needs of the time, to make new laws, to assemble together new congregations, to make an abbey of a canonry; and, on the other hand, to divide a rich bishopric and unite the poor ones.
8. That he alone may use the imperial insignia.
9. That of the pope alone all princes shall kiss the feet.
10. That his name alone shall be spoken in the churches.
11. That this title [Pope] is unique in the world.
12. That it may be permitted to him to depose emperors.
13. That he may be permitted to transfer bishops if need be.
14. That he has power to ordain a clerk of any church he may wish.
15. That he who is ordained by him may preside over another church, but may not hold a subordinate position; and that such a one may not receive a higher grade from any bishop.
16. That no synod shall be called a general one without his order.
17. That no chapter and no book shall be considered canonical without his authority.
18. That a sentence passed by him may be retracted by no one; and that he himself, alone of all, may retract it.
19. That he himself may be judged by no one.
20. That no one shall dare to condemn one who appeals to the apostolic chair.
21. That to the latter should be referred the more important cases of every church.
22. That the Roman church has never erred; nor will it err to all eternity, the Scripture bearing witness.
23. That the Roman pontiff, if he have been canonically ordained, is undoubtedly made a saint by the merits of St. Peter; St Ennodius, bishop of Pavia, bearing witness, and many holy fathers agreeing with him. As is contained in the decrees of St. Symmachus the pope.
24. That, by his command and consent, it may be lawful for subordinates to bring accusations.
25. That he may depose and reinstate bishops without assembling a synod.
26. That he who is not at peace with the Roman church shall not be considered catholic.
27. That he may absolve subjects from their fealty to wicked men.

Page 87: An extract from the Koran

Freedom from obligation [is proclaimed] from Allah and His messenger toward those of the idolaters with whom ye made a treaty.

Page 90: An extract from *The Canterbury Tales*

When April with his sweet showers
Has ended the March drought
And bathed every plant in such liquid
As will result in flowers;
When wind with his breath
Has inspired, in every wood and field,
The tender crops to grow, and the young sun
Has run half of his course into Aries
And little birds are singing,
Those who sleep all night with their eyes open
(So Nature incites them to act),
Then people wish to go on pilgrimages,
And professional pilgrims travel to foreign lands,
To distant shrines in various countries
But especially from every shire in England
People make their way to Canterbury
To seek the blessed martyr
So that he might help them in their sickness.

On one day in that season,
I was waiting in Southwark
Ready to start on my pilgrimage
To Canterbury, with feelings of devotion,
When one evening there came into the hostel
A group of 29 people
A range of people who happened to fall
Into each other's company, and they were all pilgrims
That would journey towards Canterbury;
The rooms and stables were spacious
And we were well rested there.
When the sun had gone down
I had spoken to everyone
And was part of their group
I suggested we rose early
To start our journey, which I will tell you about.
But, while I still have the chance
And before I get too far into this story,
I think it is appropriate
To tell you who they were, their social rank
And what clothing they were wearing.
I will begin with the knight.

Pages 102–103: The Canticle of Sainte Eulalie

During the story, Eulalie is subject to threats, bribes and torture at the hands of the emperor Maximian. Though she survives being burned at the stake, she is eventually decapitated before she takes the form of a dove and ascends to heaven. The first page of the document also includes some lines from the Ludwigslied, meaning Song of Ludwig, a poem written in Old High German which commemorates the victory of Louis III of France's victory over the Danish raiders during the Battle of Saucourt-en-Vimeu on 3 August 881. The Ludwigslied is written on pages within the Canticle of Saint Eulalie and appear to have been written by the same person.

Page 145: Joan of Arc's second letter to the people of Reims, 28 March 1430

Addressed: To my very dear and good friends, men of the church aldermaen, burgesses, and inhabitants and masters of the good city of Reims
Very dear and good friends, may it please you to know that I have received your letters, which mention how word had been brought to the king that within the good city of Rheims there is much evil. If you wish to know, it has, in fact, been reported that there were many who belonged to a conspiracy and who would have betrayed the city and brought in the Burgundians. But thereafter the king learned otherwise because you had sent him assurances, for which he is well pleased with you. And know that you are in his favor, and if you will have to fight, he will aid you in the event of a siege. And he well knows that you have much suffering to endure from the hardships which these treasonous Burgundian enemies inflict on you; so he will deliver you, if it pleases God, very soon - that is to say, the very soonest that he can. So I pray and request, very dear friends, that you defend the city for the King and that you keep good watch. You will soon hear my good news in greater detail. I will not write any more for the present except that all of Brittany is French, and the Duke must send three thousand soldiers to the king, paid for two months. I commend you to God, may He watch over you. Written at Sully on the 28th of March.
Jehanne